Measuring and Managing Customer Satisfaction

Also available from ASQ Quality Press

Total Quality Service: A Simplified Approach to Using the Baldrige Award Criteria
Sheila Kessler

Quality Quotes
Hélio Gomes

Customer Retention: An Integrated Process for Keeping Your Best Customers
Michael W. Lowenstein

Measuring Customer Satisfaction: Development and Use of Questionnaires
Bob E. Hayes

The Service/Quality Solution: Using Service Management to Gain Competitive Advantage
David A. Collier

To request a complimentary catalog of publications, call 800-248-1946.

Measuring and Managing Customer Satisfaction

Going for the Gold

Sheila Kessler

ASQ Quality Press
Milwaukee, Wisconsin

Measuring and Managing Customer Satisfaction: Going for the Gold
Sheila Kessler

Library of Congress Cataloging-in-Publication Data
Kessler, Sheila.
    Measuring and managing customer satisfaction: going for the gold
    / Sheila Kessler.
        p. cm.
    Includes bibliographical references and index.
    ISBN 0-87389-364-6 (alk. paper)
    1. Consumer satisfaction—Evaluation.   Title.
HF5415.335.K47   1996
658.8'12—dc20   96-19579
                                                                          CIP

10 9 8 7 6 5 4 3

ISBN 0-87389-364-6

Acquisitions Editor: Roger Holloway
Project Editor: Kelley Cardinal

ASQC Mission: To facilitate continuous improvement and increase customer satisfaction by identifying, communicating, and promoting the use of quality principles, concepts, and technologies; and thereby be recognized throughout the world as the leading authority on, and champion for, quality.

Attention: Schools and Corporations
ASQC Quality Press books, audiotapes, videotapes, and software are available at quantity discounts with bulk purchases for business, educational, or instructional use. For information, please contact ASQC Quality Press at 800-248-1946, or write to ASQC Quality Press, P.O. Box 3005, Milwaukee, WI 53201-3005.

For a free copy of the ASQC Quality Press Publications Catalog, including ASQC membership information, call 800-248-1946.

Printed in the United States of America

 Printed on acid-free recycled paper

American Society for Quality

Quality Press
611 East Wisconsin Avenue
P.O. Box 3005
Milwaukee, Wisconsin 53201-3005

Contents

Preface

The motivation to write this book was driven by a gap I felt in the literature I had read on surveys, customer satisfaction systems (CSSs), and managing customer value. After 17 years of involvement with statistics, surveys, and high-performing companies, I found some inconsistencies between what I had read, training I had attended, and what *really* made companies successful in integrating the voice of the customer to delight customers.

Written customer surveys and satisfaction measures were supposed to be the answer in the late 1970s and 1980s. Surveys did help managers and employees learn to focus on customers. Then competitive measures and pricing were introduced through an excellent model in Bradley T. Gale's book, *Managing Customer Value*. This book was a quantum leap in understanding the connection between people value added (PVA), customer value added (CVA), and economic value added (EVA). AT&T and other companies had done a terrific job of statistically showing the impact of employee well-being on customer well-being and finally on economic well-being. Perceived market value was a key indicator of growth in market share and profits. The *customer perception of value* answered the questions on price versus features compared to the competition. Competition and price were critical areas that had been systematically neglected.

Yet something was still missing. In my own experience, some of the companies best at using predictive measures for revenue and profit were not the best on the frontline. Employees were complaining instead of being excited. Interviews with customers yielded inconsistent levels of satisfaction. People at the frontline sometimes didn't know answers and didn't seem to care. How could a company have such a rigorous customer satisfaction measurement system and not have it permeate every moment of truth with customers? Yet these companies were strong technical and financial performers that were paying attention to pricing and competition. Let's call these companies the high-performing *rigorous* companies. They were definitely better than the pack. I was struck with the difference between these rigorous companies and the ones I had worked with that not only had multipoint rigorous measures, but had people, systems, and products/services that delighted shareholders, customers, and employees.

At Competitive Edge, part of our services include performing needs assessments for clients on their customers, employees, and suppliers plus. In addition, we do some "mystery shopping." Since these measures are person-to-person, they provide a good feel for the spirit of the product or service delivery process. The thousands of observations and conversations with our rigorous clients' employees, suppliers, and customers were revealing. Mystery shopping among the rigorous companies revealed high satisfaction with the product but inconsistent levels of employee and customer satisfaction with their services. We asked the high-level managers what went into PVA, CVA, and EVA, and the managers couldn't tell us, even though their bonuses were based on it. I usually heard the answer, "To tell you the truth, I'm not sure exactly what is in the formula." Talking to suppliers revealed the same inconsistencies. Frequently they told us that this high-performing company set high standards, which they respected. But the suppliers felt the company was not very service oriented with them.

I put it together. The customer satisfaction measurement system had become too scientific, too complex, and not well understood by employees. Their report card methodology was solid. Shareholders usually benefited from this predictive rigor. But the dynamic quality of the customer research—the personal touch, the employee involvement, the customer excitement—was missing. Frontline people, customers, or suppliers were not part of the input, the development of the system, or the deployment of the quality initiatives.

These rigorous companies seemed to have a vulnerability to any competitor that came along that not only had the technology but the human and user-friendly touch. Thus, a competitor could use this weakness, could easily pick off dissatisfied employees and customers, and quickly surpass them in market share. It seemed as if the high-performing, high-measurement companies had the technical, statistical, and measurement aspects down pat. What was missing was the service and commitment edge. Even though the rigorous companies may have been better than their competition in both products and services, there was a huge gap between what customers really wanted and what the entire industry was providing. The computer, electronics, telecommunications, and software industries had more than their share of rigorous companies.

In contrast were the companies with a passion for excellence. Those companies included Nordstroms, Federal Express, Milliken, MBNA, Saturn, Home Depot, Marriott, Ames Rubber, University of Phoenix, PEPCO, Johnson & Johnson, Wainwright, Armstrong, AT&T Universal Card Services, Solectron, Schwab, Marlow, and many other lesser-known companies. Let's call these the *going-for-the-gold* companies. Some weren't as scientific about their written measures, but spent much more time *talking to customers, listening to employees, watching customers use their products, and developing partnerships with key accounts.* The hearts, souls, and heads of the frontline people demonstrated their customer concern. They truly listened. Managers listened to employees *and* customers. Managers hired the right people and gave them the right systems, training, and resources they needed to attend to customers.

The going-for-the-gold companies were not only financially successful, but sustained that success (whether they were manufacturing or service companies). They had fiercely loyal customers that would be tough for a competitor to steal. Few surveys have included a fierce loyalty issue. As we looked at the last 15 years of financial performance, the going-for-the-gold CSS companies had a more consistent level of performance and higher stock returns than did the rigorous companies. The type of industry didn't matter. Each industry—electronics, hotels, engineering, distribution, utilities, car manufacturers, transportation, retail, auto dealers, financial institutions, insurance, credit cards, building supplies, health care, and education—had its own examples of going-for-the-gold category killers.

In my workshops on customer retention, I ask participants to draw a picture of the satisfaction level of their employees, customers, and shareholders on flip-chart paper. Later we dip into left-brain measurements; the pictures capture the spirit as well as the trend. Most of the participants are vice presidents or managers of marketing, customer service, manufacturing, operations, sales, marketing research, and the like. They are usually from Fortune 500 firms, midsize companies, and health care. About 10 percent draw three happy faces. The other 90 percent talk about happy shareholders but unhappy employees, happy customers but unhappy shareholders, and so on.

The key difference between three happy faces and just one or two seemed to be in more dynamic, more personal measures, with more focus on fixes than report cards. Customers and employees were also involved in the CSS. Multiple listening posts, ownership of fixes, systematic review, and a positive approach were also key. The gold CSS companies also seemed to have employees who were highly informed about financial, quality, customer satisfaction, and employee measures. Rigor may create excellence and shareholder satisfaction; rigor *and* passion seem to make companies irresistible—to their employees, customers, and shareholders. The purpose of this book is to share the collective CSS stories of those gold companies with *three* happy faces, not just one.

Target Audience for This Book

This book was written for people in high-tech, high-touch, high-stakes, or high-ticket organizations. Most of these executives, managers, or employees are working on partnering with key customers. Examples include telecommunications, distribution, banks, investors, retail, fast food, transportation, hospitality, computers, software, grocery, software, education, health care, engineering, government, customized manufacturing, or any organization with direct customer contact (whether distributors or end users). Customers can be internal or external.

Understanding your customers does not depend on the size of your unit or company. The going-for-the-gold CSS has increased business in a dental office with 10 employees. It has also increased revenues for a $16 billion company. Small companies can have data underload or overload, as can large companies. This book is designed to help devise a rigorous, yet simple system that pulls input from many sources, but integrates the data in a decision-friendly way. It takes a step-by-step approach to planning, implementing, and getting results. The tool tip section in Part IV provides a ready reference on how to use the tools and specific tips from the collective successes of gold CSS companies. These tools include customer satisfaction surveys, focus groups, lost customer surveys, transaction surveys, analysis and synthesis tools, all the way to celebrations.

This book is not designed to be a comprehensive, statistical how-to book. If executives, managers, and employees can have a fundamental grasp on designing a CSS, implementing it with the spirit of the customers and employees behind it, and synthesizing the data, this book will have done enough. The book also does not focus on traditional, statistically oriented consumer research on packaged goods. Most college marketing courses have plenty of excellent information on consumer research and marketing. This book focuses on the more neglected side of the formula—how to measure *and manage* customer satisfaction and value for businesses that sell to other businesses, and deliver high-tech, high-touch, high-stakes, and high-ticket services or products. The gold measurement systems are meant to be used with gold clients—ones with whom you are trying to partner.

Acknowledgments

I would like to credit many people for their contributions to this book. Noriaki Kano, whom I met and got to know in Japan, made a profound difference in my thinking. He graciously gave permission to use his quality model as the framework for the measurement and management system in this book. W. Edwards Deming, in the seminars I attended with him and the work I saw him doing with Procter & Gamble, Zytec, and parts of General Motors, was also a strong force in helping me focus on customer-driven systems. Those systems included areas that were harder to fix, such as hiring, training, promotions, designing new products, compensation systems, communication with customers and employees, and information infrastructure. In addition, Doug Tersteeg, who, as the quality manager, led Zytec to the Malcolm Baldrige National Quality Award in 1991, contributed his depth of understanding in translating customer needs into highly technical products.

I also owe a great deal to both the Marriott and Delta managers and employees who helped me understand how you can really hook customers. Neither was perfect; both were a quantum leap above their competitors in my own *very* extensive experience with them. As an advisory board member for Delta, I greatly respected the company's ability to listen to and integrate customer feedback.

Many thanks go to those companies who have both used my systems and ideas, and contributed their own in the process. Those companies include Motorola, Hughes, Boeing, Microsoft, Fluor Daniel, AT&T, Corning, Halliburton, Delta, Marriott, Bell South, Golden State Foods (food processor and distributor for McDonald's), Nordstrom's, Taco Bell, Coca-Cola, Toshiba, FHP, Humana, and many others. The world-class people I worked with in these organizations kept the bar moving higher and higher.

Another company that deserves special mention is Prism Radio Partners. Backed by J.P. Morgan, Bill Phalen, the chief executive officer bought 16 radio stations in five cities and used service quality as the competitive edge. I helped the company design its gold CSS, which was launched shortly after the birth of the company. Mike Cutchall, the chief operating officer, transformed the sales force from a cutthroat, used-car-sales approach to one that focused on partnering and getting results for advertisers. The results from the multipoint, rigorous research were integrated in strategic quality planing and were used to design new management and sales training programs, hiring practices, promotions, and a new compensation system. In less than three years, Prism tripled its market value for J.P. Morgan and merged with the largest radio conglomerate in the United States. In less than three years, Prism had redefined radio to advertisers and listeners. As a consultant, I was honored to be an integral part of that transformation. A gold CSS was the centerpiece, managed by one very competent woman, Marci Joyce. It was truly a customer-driven company.

Last but not least, many thanks are due to Nancy Kishishita, my administrative assisstant, who not only worked all night several times to make deadlines but also provided helpful feedback on the copy of this book.

Also, my husband, Barry Halsted, deserves an enormous amount of credit. He is gifted with his ability to combine technical expertise, alternative tactics, and common sense to design solutions that work for clients. His persistence in getting the job done for customers is one of the highest standards I have seen. His strong partnership with customers has always enhanced revenues and profits at the companies for which he has worked. Integrity is the key word. And with my work overload, extensive travel, and little sleep, I greatly appreciate his patience, love, and support, without which I would not have had the energy to write this book.

Part I

The Customer Satisfaction System Plan

Going-for-the-Gold CSS

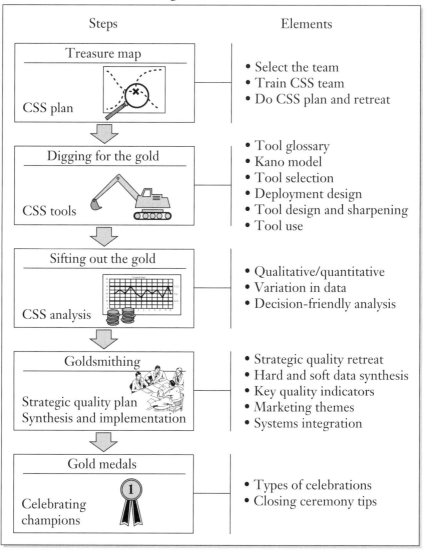

Steps	Elements
Treasure map CSS plan	• Select the team • Train CSS team • Do CSS plan and retreat
Digging for the gold CSS tools	• Tool glossary • Kano model • Tool selection • Deployment design • Tool design and sharpening • Tool use
Sifting out the gold CSS analysis	• Qualitative/quantitative • Variation in data • Decision-friendly analysis
Goldsmithing Strategic quality plan Synthesis and implementation	• Strategic quality retreat • Hard and soft data synthesis • Key quality indicators • Marketing themes • Systems integration
Gold medals Celebrating champions	• Types of celebrations • Closing ceremony tips

Chapter 1

Introduction to Going for the Gold

Many executives, managers, employees, and researchers are scratching their heads wondering, "Why doesn't our customer satisfaction survey predict financial growth?" "Why do some of our customers seem irritated with the survey process?" "Why do the results sit on the shelf?" *Measuring and Managing Customer Satisfaction: Going for the Gold* describes a dynamic, user-friendly, multipoint, and yet predictive system for measuring and managing customer satisfaction that works to improve customer satisfaction, perceived market value, employee satisfaction, and shareholder satisfaction. The planning, tools, and systems necessary in a gold customer satisfaction system (CSS) are distilled from the best of the best in diverse industries. This chapter details the first profound question, "Why bother?"

- Current trends
- The need for an integrated customer satisfaction system
- New applications for customer satisfaction research
- Benefits of using a going-for-the-gold CSS
- Satisfaction and market share
- Satisfaction data as an early warning sign
- How much will a gold CSS cost?

Current Trends

Customer focus and satisfaction is a driving force for organizations gearing up for surviving or thriving in the twenty-first century. Those that are truly doing it have turned into consistently high performers, for example, Milliken, Motorola, Nordstroms, Home Depot, Marriott, Marlow, Solectron, and AT&T Universal Card Services. These companies emphasize service quality in their strategy, giving customers what they want, when they want it, and how they want it. They train their frontline employees well and measure customer satisfaction. Why is measurement such an important part of a customer satisfaction system?

> *If you are not measuring it, you are not managing it.*

The main ingredient? A zealous respect for the value of customer satisfaction real time, every time, *and* an understanding of how to gather, analyze, and use customer data to increase business. Which features will customers be willing to pay more for? Which features can you eliminate to lower the price? How much are customers willing to spend to receive the item in hours instead of days or in days instead of weeks? What causes customers to be loyal advocates of your product or service rather than just consumers?

Fine-tuning your measurement tools is also a challenge. You may find yourself asking some or all of these questions: Do we use a written survey once a year? Do we call of our customers on the telephone? Do we sample all of our customers, or just focus on the top-tier customers? How can we make our questions more actionable? What can we do to make sure the company uses, rather than swims in, the data? Should we include competitors' clients? How do we recruit them if we want to use them? How do we know that customer satisfaction measures will increase either revenue or market share?

All these questions are answered in this book. The going-for-the-gold model of a CSS overcomes most of the deficiencies of previous poorly designed CSSs. The key is to put as much rigor into your CSS as you do into your financial measurement systems. Even though measurement is considered a research function, you are also managing the perception of your entire company as a result of how you do research. It's not that difficult to do it right. A little focus on both up-front planning and downstream implementation makes the difference.

The Need for an Integrated Customer Satisfaction System

Overall, the systematic effort to "know the customer" is just beginning in the United States. According to Jim Findlay, market researcher at Information Resources in Chicago, "72 percent of all products fail after an average of $15 million has been spent to produce them."[1] This is after all the market research has been done. More than $3.5 billion a year are spent with the 50 biggest market research firms in the United States.

Why such a poor record? Many companies count too much on surveys—too superficial. Many companies count too much on focus groups—too few numbers to extrapolate. Many companies haven't learned how to design good metrics or how to deal with or integrate multiple sources of customer data. Most companies haven't related their soft satisfaction data with the hard truths at the cash register. The uses of solid customer feedback are unlimited.

New Applications for Customer Satisfaction Research

In addition to using CSS results for training, hiring, compensation, and strategic quality planning, other needs for solid results are evident. A rather dramatic example of how customer satisfaction data could have prevented a huge financial bungle was demonstrated when Converse bought Apex.[2]

Converse Shoe Company trumpeted the purchase of Apex One on May 18, 1995. By August 11, 1995 it closed the doors of Apex, the very company that had been a dream buy. At the time of purchase, both companies were financially highly successful. Converse saw a winner in Apex's financial statements because Apex had been a "jewel of the sports apparel industry." The only problem was that dissatisfied customers were about to bolt at the time of the sale. Right after the sale, they did bolt. The dissatisfied customers were all the retailers who hadn't received their Apex shipments in time for the sports seasons in previous years.

The retailers had put up with poor order fulfillment for two years, and the third year was the breaking point for their frustrations. They defected, just in time for the sale. Within 85 days, Apex's compounded financial problems forced Converse to close down Apex. This closure was one of the fastest downward spirals in history. If Converse had done some customer satisfaction research in its due diligence process, it would have detected the early warning signs. The financial investment community also needs to include customer assessment as part of due diligence.

The use for customer satisfaction data stretches from financing products, product and service design, product or service launch, refinements in services and products, and selling a unit or company, to marketing the customer-perceived strengths of the service or product. Companies or products can crash on *any* one of these points.

Benefits of Using a Going-for-the-Gold CSS

How do we know that this level of customer focus has been profitable to date? It sometimes requires taking risks, tapping automation, training employees, using flexible thinking, and designing innovative processes. It requires extensive knowledge of the customer that was more prevalent in nineteenth-century small towns. The evidence is all around us.

Sweden has a national Customer Satisfaction Index that Claes Fornell created in 1989. It measures more than 100 companies in Sweden. Fornell said that an increase in customer satisfaction of just one point is noteworthy. For the typical Swedish firm with an asset base of $600 million, the total value of an annual one-point increase in customer satisfaction over a five-year span is worth more than cumulative incremental returns of 16.66% (relative total current return on investment). With a total increase of five points over a five-year period, the average American firm would net $94 million in cumulative incremental return.[3]

AT&T's research demonstrated that changes in customer value—either in quality, price, or both—were followed in only a few months by changes in customer perceptions and only a few months after that by changes in market share.[4] The sequence of how this chain reaction goes is shown in Exhibit 1.1. AT&T finds a four-month lag in each step between improvements in quality, customer perception of quality, and market share. Federal Express says its cycle is more like 48 hours.[5]

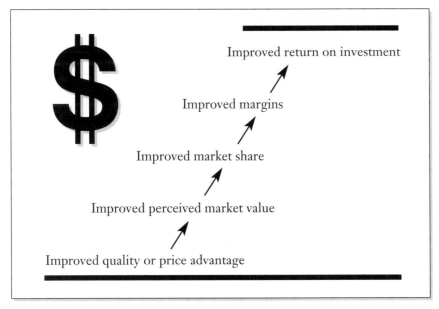

Exhibit 1.1   Quality and profitability market share.

Satisfaction and Market Share

Similar relationships were shown on a larger scale. The profit impact of market strategy (PIMS) program is managed by the Strategic Planning Institute (SPI) in Cambridge, Massachusetts. SPI and university researchers used data from 2746 business units to study relationships between market strategies and business results. Their research showed a strong relationship between superior quality and return on investment.[6]

Businesses with superior quality average about 30 percent return on investment.

Businesses with inferior quality average a mere 10 percent.

You may think all this doesn't make that much difference. After all, it is *just* a customer satisfaction survey. Take a look at how competitive the world has become. Each one of these moments of truth where the customer encounters the organization influences the overall satisfaction level. Let's take three companies with three different customer satisfaction measurement scores at the start.

Company A   99 percent

Company B   98 percent

Company C   95 percent

All three ratings seem outstanding. If you were to extend buying decisions over time, though, you would find that people gravitate toward the more satisfying company.[7] Say an employee of Company C irritates a customer. The customer defects, but is more sophisticated now in shopping. The individual picks Company B. A set of irritants opens the individual to shopping again. The person is even more sophisticated and asks better questions. Company A is the answer. Look at Exhibit 1.2 to see what happens to market share among the

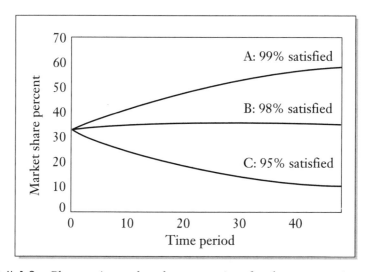

Exhibit 1.2   Changes in market share over time for three competitors with equal initial market share.

Source: Pete Babrich, "Customer Satisfaction: How Good Is Good Enough," *Quality Progress* 25, no. 12 (December 1992): 66.

three competitors if they all started with a 33 percent market share. Over 24 time periods, Company A, with a respectable satisfaction rating of 99 percent, ends up with a 60 percent market share. Company C, also with a respectable satisfaction rating of 95 percent, ends up with 10 percent market share. That can be disastrous.

Likewise, word of mouth from satisfied customers has become an increasingly important part of any marketing strategy. I use both Delta and Marriott, my two travel quality partners, as examples in keynote speeches to tens of thousands of people every year. They happen to be a source of many positive examples of how to retain customers. Their standard makes it tough for me to put up with less in a travel schedule that consumes 80 percent of my time.

Word of mouth is considerably more powerful than advertising. The believability of advertising messages has markedly decreased in the last decade. Every day an individual is bombarded with at least 2500 advertising messages. The trust level of advertising has gone from 55 percent to 12 percent in the last five years. At least 50 percent of all college students now take a marketing course. In order to give your message a chance of getting through, you have to focus. Advertising messages were believed by only 8 percent of people in 1994.[8] Your loyal customers become a free and yet powerful extension of your sales and marketing people, thus lowering your cost of sales. But your customer assessment system has to please customers while it assesses them. That is why taking the tips in this book seriously is so important.

Satisfaction Data as an Early Warning Sign

Consider the impact of not looking at customer satisfaction data. Customer satisfaction data provide early warning signs of problems before they show up in revenue and profit downturns. Exhibit 1.3 illustrates increasingly traumatic stages of internal problems.

At first, a problem like inadequate tools or a poor manager can overheat the engine. You can spot difficulties when employee satisfaction and quality measures go down and employee attrition goes up. Rework increases and employees become discouraged. These measures are called people value added (PVA) in Bradley T. Gale's book, *Managing Customer Value*.[9] If managers are watching the instrument panel, they see the oil getting hot and the pressure low. A soft landing is possible with early repair and little damage to the plane.

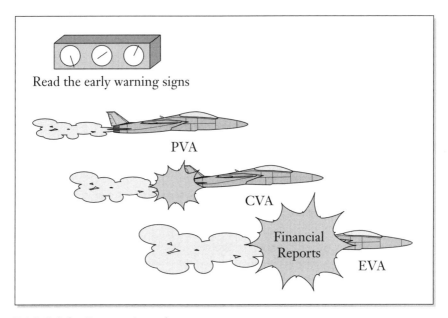

Exhibit 1.3   Progression of events.

If no one is watching the instrument panel or if too few instruments are provided, stage two sets in. The flames grow, the plane's damage increases, and customers start feeling it. Gale calls this customer value added (CVA). Service goes down. Employees vent their frustrations and become distracted. The perceived market value of the product or service goes down in the customer's mind and customer attrition goes up. Damage to the plane increases. Repairs are more costly and difficult. Landing and repairs are still possible.

The final stage shows up on the financial measures, economic value added (EVA). By the time the problems show up in revenues and profits, the plane may be so damaged that a death spiral is imminent. Corrective action may mean having to transfer or fire someone or shut down a unit. Customers have defected as a result and are not easily retrieved. Revenues and profits have plummeted. The point? PVA leads to CVA, which leads to EVA. Someone needs to be watching the cockpit instrument panel for early warning signs in employee and customer satisfaction before it shows up on the bottom line. That is why *multiple* customer listening posts are vital.

This death spiral can tumble an organization in short order. Huge giants become pathetic giants. Grant Department Stores, I-Magnin, Braniff, National Lumber, Pan Am, Eastern Airlines, and dozens of others are but a few examples of companies that didn't bother to build this feedback bridge with their customers and then act on the data.

The intervals between these stages vary according to the intervals between purchase decisions for customers. Fast food customers eat at their favorite place three to five times a week;[10] the timing between poor PVA, CVA, and EVA can be weeks. Cars, boats, insurance policies, and health care policies represent longer buying cycles; the timing can be years. The shorter the interval, the closer the interval between PVA, CVA, and EVA.

Some divisions of AT&T have scientifically refined Gale's model to detect early warning signs as predictors of financial success. Manager and employee bonuses are based on a formula for managing all three. Still, substantial differences exist between many of the divisions within AT&T and how they apply their tools. The issues are (1) how many tools are used, (2) how the tools are developed, (3) how much customers and employees are involved in the development and deployment of the instruments and results, and (4) how the results are integrated and deployed. AT&T Universal Card Services has the system that is closest to gold. It hires with customer needs in mind. It uses the data to train people. It has varied listening posts with frequent review and ownership of issues, and a positive rather than punitive attitude toward results prevails.

The test comes in mystery shopping. At truly gold companies, the frontline people have the answers, are motivated to solve problems, and seem happy. Their suppliers concur. They have combined science with art. They have combined measuring with *managing* customer satisfaction.

How Much Will a Gold CSS Cost?

A gold CSS will make money, not cost money in the long term. Immediate revenues can be found in lost customer research. Many clients I work with now track their target customers, one by one. They can easily measure the revenue and profit growth as a result of their focus on customer value.

You would be very rich if you had invested in the mid-1980s in many of the high-performing companies mentioned in this book. They have all outperformed the Standards & Poors.

How to Use This Book

The chapters in the book follow the CSS model in Exhibit 1.4. The secret is not only in what to do, but in how to do it. Part I (chapters 1–3), covers the reasons behind the CSS, the problems and opportunities, and the CSS plan or treasure map.

Part II (chapters 4–6) highlights the selection of tools, refining those tools, and using them. Chapter 4, Selecting Your Tools, will help you understand and select the appropriate tools, for example, complaint handling, customer satisfaction, advisory groups, focus groups, observation, and so on. Chapter 5, Sharpening Your Tools, discusses the nuances of using your selected tools. The deployment and use of the tools is covered in chapter 6, Using the Tools.

Part III (chapters 7–9) covers analyzing and synthesizing data. Sifting through the dirt and retrieving the gold nuggets is the mainstay of chapter 7, Sifting Out the Gold. Chapter 8 helps you master customer goldsmithing—how to turn those nuggets into valuable items through the strategic quality planning process. Chapter 9 focuses on celebrating your gold champions. Visibility and recognition for progress are vital.

Part IV (Chapters 10–12) is a tool tip section for tools listed in previous chapters. The tools in the tool tip section are listed in three parts.

1. Chapter 10: Tools for Gathering Data, for example, surveys, focus groups, and so on

2. Chapter 11: Tools for Designing, Analyzing, and Synthesizing Data, such as control charts and graphs

3. Chapter 12: Tools for Using the Data, for example, quality improvement teams and celebrations

Each of the three chapters covers the tools in alphabetical order for ease of reference.

This book places an emphasis on the planning and implementation phases of CSS. The book will also help you understand several tools that

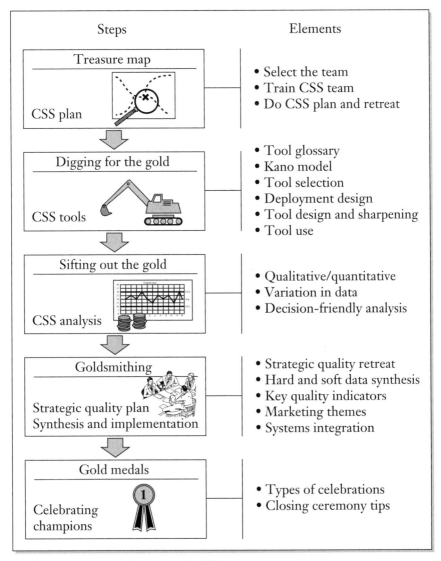

Exhibit 1.4   Going-for-the-gold CSS.

can be more powerful than a written questionnaire, for example, focus interviews, lost customer surveys, transaction reports, and complaint tracking. If you need more help on the written questionnaire, Bob E. Hayes' book, *Measuring Customer Satisfaction: Development and Use of Questionnaires* is an excellent book on questionnaire design.[11] Likewise, if you are not familiar with statistics, you might recruit someone to help you with the statistical pieces like sampling and variation. This book is written primarily for executives, managers, and employees who are not statisticians. Everyone involved in measuring and managing customer satisfaction needs to be familiar with the simple statistical concepts so your system is scientific. You can enlist a few hours of help from a statistician to design the sample size and do the number crunching.

Notes

1. Pollack Tudann, "Role of new products puts scope on SKUs," *Advertising Age*, 9 October 1995, 18.

2. Mark Maremount, "How Converse Got Its Laces All Tangled: It Lost $42.6 Million in 85 Days on Clothing Maker Apex One," *Business Week*, 4 September 1995.

3. Jon Brecka, "The American Customer Satisfaction Index," *Quality Progress* 27, no. 10 (October 1994): 4.

4. Bradley T. Gale, *Managing Customer Value* (New York: Free Press, 1994), 304.

5. Raymond Kordupleski, "Setting Standards for Tracking Relative Customer Value, Quality, and Price" (speech given at ASQC's 7th Annual Customer Satisfaction and Quality Measurement Conference, Dallas, Texas, 21 February 1995).

6. Gale, *Managing Customer Value*, 308.

7. Pete Babrich, "Customer Satisfaction: How Good Is Good Enough," *Quality Progress* 25, no. 12 (December 1992): 65–68.

8. *Communication Briefings* (newsletter), November 1994.

9. Gale, *Managing Customer Value*.

10. Radio Advertising Bureau, *Instant Backgrounds* (New York: Radio Advertising Bureau, February 1996).

11. Bob E. Hayes, *Measuring Customer Satisfaction: Development and Use of Questionnaires* (Milwaukee: ASQC Quality Press, 1992).

Chapter 2

Problems and Opportunities with Current Customer Satisfaction Measurement

This chapter first covers the problems, then the opportunities, that exist with the current state-of-the-art systems for measuring and managing customer satisfaction. Just as early treasure maps had dragons where the sailors knew there was danger, this chapter will point out the dragons. The primary CSS problems are the following:

- Does too little, too late
- Doesn't include information about competitors
- Doesn't focus on important customers
- Doesn't match the depth of the tool to the sophistication of customers
- Is designed at too low a level in the organization
- Fails to see that you are managing perception while you are measuring it
- Doesn't take pricing into account
- Doesn't test the tools before deploying them
- Settles for too small a response rate

The starting point will be the problems.

Problems

Does Too Little, Too Late

The problem with a once-a-year written survey was discussed in chapter 1. That doesn't mean throw it out. It does mean one survey isn't enough. It is typically too little, too late to truly be responsive to dynamic market conditions. No matter what your company size, you need to have a simple but comprehensive system for keeping ahead of your competition. As you read this book, you can pick the tools that will be most useful to your type of business and your priority customers. A one-size system does not fit all.

Contrast this once-a-year style with Honda. In November 1992, factory workers who actually bolt and bang the Accord together called more than 47,000 recent Accord buyers, or about half of the owners who registered their cars that year. They were looking for ideas for improvements.[1]

Doesn't Include Information About Competitors

A second problem with the written survey is that few companies are getting good measures of competitive data. The buying decision is ultimately determined not by how good you are, but by how good you are relative to your competition. The early-1990s performance of Pan Am, IBM, General Motors, Digital Equipment, and other giants attests to the price of not keeping up with competitors.

In order to get good competitive data, a survey needs to include your competitor's customers as well as your own in a perceptual study (see chapter 10). Perceptual studies require neutral outside companies. Organizations like J.D. Powers perform large-scale competitive comparisons on the auto industry. Competitive Edge does the same thing for business-to-business organizations. Business-to-business organizations may be consumer goods businesses, but a key part of their business is their distribution channel—resellers, retailers, distribution companies, and so on.

At a minimum, you can get limited competitive data by including questions about your competitors in a customer satisfaction survey or in a focus group. The customer satisfaction survey part of the tool tip section provides an illustration. Remember you are asking *your* key customers questions about your competitors. That is different from asking *your competitors'* key customers questions about you. You usually get very different results. If you want to increase your business, you need to know why customers choose your competitors over you. Some comparative data is better than none, though.

Doesn't Focus on Important Customers

Many companies send a survey to a sample of all of their customers. The problem with that tactic is everyone ends up with an equal vote. The next chapter will demonstrate how to segment your customer base and focus on those segments that are linked closely to your future financial success. Without this strategic focus, your CSS can lead to decisions that can actually *decrease* your target customers' satisfaction and therefore decrease your profits.

Doesn't Match the Depth of the Tool to the Sophistication of Customers

The sophistication of the tool needs to match the sophistication and profit potential of the customer base. Using a $6-an-hour college student to interview managers or executives may just irritate them as they realize that they are just a number in a study. Using that same liberal arts student to ask questions about high technology doesn't allow any technical probing. Using a short written survey to measure satisfaction for a hospital Board of Directors just communicates your lack of interest in what they have to say.

For large packaged goods or consumer companies with millions of customers, this may be a difficult financial decision. The answer is simple. You don't have to sample all your customers. Spend more money sampling your big ticket customers, such as distributors, resellers, and national channels. Eastman Kodak first looked at its dealers and found it had 6375 of them—which made it a bit difficult to do comprehensive research. Looking more closely, it determined that 128 customers were responsible for 89 percent of the revenues. That made it much easier to target key customers with a more personal and robust CSS.[2] Spend less measuring your low-profit customers. You spend the same total amount of money, but will gain deeper insights in how to become more attractive to those customers that will make you financially successful.

Many technical companies like Eastman Kodak and Corning use neutral outsiders to interview their key customers. Other well-known power supply companies, electronic firms, phone companies, and utilities we have worked with use internal researchers to do the same. If the products are technical or services are complex, the interviewer needs to be highly trained in the product or service lines, the competition, and the critical features. If you use internal researchers, the researchers need considerable up-front training and monitoring in interview skills. This train-the-internal-interviewer approach works much better than delegating customer satisfaction research on sophisticated products or services to an outside mass-marketing research firm. Several electronics and satellite firms we work with use a neutral research group within the company to do the calling. These interviewers are rigorously selected and highly trained. The position is considered a launching pad to higher management.

Is Designed at Too Low a Level in the Organization

Many of the CSSs are designed by a manager of customer service or marketing or even human resources. A team may be involved. The problem at this level is that each manager feels inhibited about coordinating his or her effort with the rest of the organization. Unless a cross-functional team or an executive sponsor can traverse these lines, the CSS will be doomed to finding little nuggets of departmental gold. A going-for-the-gold CSS is just what it says. If integrated at the top, it sets you up to mine the mother lode.

The mother lode approach in improving customer satisfaction is found at high altitudes. Unless people at the top of the unit are willing to be involved, I suggest that you either lower your expectations for what can be achieved or don't do satisfaction research at all. Commitment from the head of the department (assuming the system just applies to your department) is the very least you need for success. Little commitment at the top will show up when you try to get the resources necessary to turn your CSS results into corrective action. You can't fake customer focus from the executive level. Don't let your executives entirely delegate this task to you if you are at an intermediate or lower level.

The book, *Total Quality Service* provides a template for a project charter.[3] A project charter can help a CSS steering committee detail the mission, objectives, and resources needed for designing and implementing a successful CSS plan. Many companies also have an executive committee that guides the company. If the CSS steering committee and executive committee are different groups, someone from the executive committee with a lot of clout needs to be involved in the CSS steering committee. Linking the two is important.

Fails to See That You Are Managing Perception While You Are Measuring It

The statistics of design have been covered well in the literature. The psychology of the measurement system needs to be as carefully considered as the sampling error. The psychology means, "What impact will this measurement tool have on either the customer, the employee, or both?"

For example, when I ordered a piece of software, I received the package by courier without a receipt. There was a "Quality Hot Line" 800 number on the box, so I called it to obtain a receipt. The woman who answered the phone said, "I have no idea how to get a receipt. They just hired me last month and they didn't train me at all. I am a temp and haven't a clue what is happening. Just call the general number and see if you can find out from the receptionist." That was the Quality Hot Line? I sent the product back. That tiny window into the rest of the organization made me wonder about the rigor of the product. Any contact you have with a customer via a measurement or complaint system is a moment of truth in how seriously you care about customers. If you don't do it right, don't do it! It is better not to create those heightened expectations.

Another Detroit automotive marketing telephone survey went through a detailed list of multiple choice questions that focused on what would get me to switch from my current car to its brand. It asked about design, 0–60 acceleration, quietness, and so on. After 20 minutes, the interviewer mentioned she had only one question left. I asked her, "You really haven't asked me anything about the area that is most critical to me in purchasing a car. Do you want to know what that is?" She said, "No, I don't have any room on my questionnaire." Okay. I never did tell her that reliability was my number one criteria. The survey questions were well designed. They were not ambiguous. Their quantitative answers lead to making predictions scientifically. She asked one question at a time. The survey just didn't include questions that would have an impact on the company's bottom line. I also extrapolated about the rigor of its product design from that simple survey. The results would be used to make major strategic decisions and determine how millions of dollars would be spent. The interviewer also didn't probe to find out whether I was an extremely loyal customer to my current brand and what my intentions were about buying a new product. This book will address the importance of that information when rolling the data into design, production, and marketing decisions. The tools you use and how you use them reflect both the precision of your company and the caring for your customers. Asking the wrong questions is one of the major customer irritants with CSSs.

The measurement tools you use or don't use say a lot about how seriously you take your customers and the quality of your service or products. The worst thing you can do is to be superficial about measuring customer satisfaction. Customers are bright. They see right through the hypocrisy and actually devalue your product or service.

Customer satisfaction = Results – Expectations

High expectations and low results lead to low customer satisfaction scores. If you pay $6000 for a business class ticket on United to Tokyo, you expect decent service. If you receive less than what you expected, your satisfaction score might be low. If you pay $49 to fly Southwest on a short flight, you don't expect much. Southwest doesn't promise much. If Southwest delivers a little fun on the airplane, and you have a tiny "wow" experience, the satisfaction score may be higher than United's. Expectations set you up to be satisfied or dissatisfied.

Your measurement system actually sends a message that you care about customers and what they want. Expectations go up. If your customer survey omits vital questions, uses questions that are biased, or asks questions in a confusing manner, you have actually done damage with your customers.

Customer surveys are windows into
the rigor of the rest of your company.

A brief quiz of the rigor of your current customer satisfaction measurement system is provided in Exhibit 2.1. For each question, place a check in the box if the answer is yes.

Customer Satisfaction Measurement Excellence Quiz

❑ 1. Do you have qualifying information on the survey to determine with what frequency your customer uses your service/product?

❑ 2. Do you have a return rate of more than 80%?

❑ 3. Are data from the survey tied into your strategic quality planning process?

❑ 4. Do you look at the data from your survey, data from your key quality measures, and purchase data all at the same time?

❑ 5. Are your key quality measures derived from customer feedback?

❑ 6. Do you have an overall satisfaction question on your questionnaire?

❑ 7. Did you use focus groups of customers to determine which questions were important to track in your satisfaction surveys?

❑ 8. Are customer needs related to what people are willing to pay for them?

❑ 9. Did you test your survey to find out whether your questions all mean the same thing to different customers?

❑ 10. Did you test the survey for management biases?

❑ 11. Do you qualify your respondents in terms of their intent to buy?

❑ 12. Do you ask questions in a way that ensures full honesty?

❑ 13. Do you use either telephone or in-person interviews to probe?

❑ 14. Have you worked out a plan so that immediate problems get fixed immediately and systems issues are tackled on a systematic basis?

❑ 15. Are lost customers' reasons for leaving tracked?

Exhibit 2.1   Customer satisfaction measurement excellence.

A score of 10–14 means you are on the right track in CSS. Fewer than that means you may want to incorporate some of the ideas in this book.

Doesn't Take Pricing Into Account

Individuals may be highly satisfied with the product but do not want to pay a high price for it. The major airlines (Delta, United, American, US Air) found this in 1993. Domestic airlines carried 450 million passengers in 1993. From 1990–1994, domestic airlines lost more money than they had made in their entire history ($12 billion).

> *If on every flight those airlines flew in the last four years,
> every ticket sold for just $10 more,
> the airlines would have made money.
> Or, if every flight had just two more passengers. Just two
> more...[4]*

Meanwhile, Southwest Airlines made $52 million while the other airlines were crashing financially. Most readers will recognize Southwest as the low-cost, no-frills airline that has been leapfrogging the industry. Even though Delta had highly satisfied both travel agents and business travelers, they were choosing the lower-cost alternative.

Thus, it is critical that the company understands how much the customer will pay for which features. In interviewing more than 120 of Delta's first-class customers, I found that they were willing to pay $100 more for extra service for a cross-country ticket, but not three times what they would pay on a comparable airline. Likewise, when Delta was looking at ways to get its passenger costs down from 9.5¢ to 7.5¢ per passenger mile, Delta asked its advisory board what customers really didn't need. Most customers wanted ease of moving through the airport, such as short lines, priority boarding, and priority baggage handling. They did not care about being served food on flights of less than an hour.

Marriott did two years' worth of research on its business travelers when it built the Courtyard. It needed to know what its traditional guests would give up to spend only $69/night instead of $129/night in a Marriott. Guests wanted clean, ample rooms and a coffee shop. They did not care about bellhops, fancy restaurants, or large ballrooms. Thus, customer needs were built into the design of the mid-price-range Courtyard. Involving customers in facility design is becoming an increasing part of customer needs assessment and satisfaction measures. Chapter 4 details how to design a winning customer satisfaction system.

Pricing calibrations are vital in developing services and products that are faster, better, and cheaper.

Doesn't Test the Tools Before Deploying Them

Even though your questions make sense to you, they may be ambiguous to your customers. Most companies develop their own jargon that customers may not understand. The best wording comes from your customers. Check for ambiguity, bias in your questions, and customer language. You need to ask only 10–15 customers to take your survey and give you feedback on what they understand from the questions.

Settles for Too Small a Response Rate

Don't settle for the typical 20 percent to 30 percent response rate on your survey. You will need to do something special to get a higher response rate. You can increase your return rate by making the survey short (two pages maximum), coding the survey and following up with nonreturns, or offering incentives for filling it out (drawings or discount coupons to your business). A hotel, airline, restaurant, grocery store, or any other public place of business will want surveys located in a prominent and easily accessible place. Training employees to ask people to fill them out will also increase the response rate.

Take a look the next time you are in a fast food or regular restaurant, bank, grocery store, or hotel. First, do they have a customer satisfaction form? Second, if they do, fill it out and ask where you should put it. Does the employee even know? Third, see what kind of response you get, if any. Most of these customer satisfaction surveys are really complaint systems for very unhappy customers.

Opportunities

The going-for-the-gold CSS has repeated themes. In addition to the step-by-step model, these themes weave their way throughout the system. These themes for success are

- A strategic focus
- Partnerships with customers and employees

- A passion for excellence
- Mass customization
- Real-time, every time customer satisfaction

A Strategic Focus

A strategic focus means that the CSS takes high-profit or high-growth segments of the business more seriously than low-profit or low-vapor-on-the-mirror (nearly dead) services or products. Chapter 3 will show how to focus your customer satisfaction efforts on strategically important customers.

Customer satisfaction data also need to be linked to financial data. The chapter on strategic quality planning (chapter 8) will help you understand how to tie the two together. You want to make sure that increases in customer satisfaction are tied to increases in revenue and profitability.

Most companies we have worked with have separate departments doing separate measurements. The customer service department usually has a complaint handling system, the marketing and sales department details which customer segments are profitable and growing, and the controllers and financial people know budgets and forecasts. The quality control department charts conformance to requirements. Customer satisfaction data come from sales or customer service. Integrating these pieces of information allows for quantum leaps in performance. That integration happens through the CSS steering committee and plan (chapter 3) and through strategic quality planning (chapter 8).

Partnerships with Customers and Employees

In a gold CSS, customers and employees are integrally involved in intelligence gathering, product launching, designing survey questions, testing tools, and the implementation process. The digging for the gold (chapter 4, tools) and goldsmithing (in chapter 8) sections will talk specifically about how to obtain that involvement efficiently and effectively.

Frontline employees are used as intelligent gatherers in a gold CSS. My experience with Japanese companies over a period of 15 years is filled with examples of how they systematically gather and analyze the information that associates, agents, or salespeople pick up every day. One illustration was when I visited Japan in the mid-1980s and landed in Tokyo. By the time I got to Osaka two days later, the Japanese knew all of my preferences on food, sports, hotels, drinks, and so on. The translator in Tokyo had diligently communicated these nuances to the counterparts in Osaka. Many Japanese companies with which I have worked have pictures of their customers in a book with all of their preferences listed. Many of the business meetings I have attended in Japan also had a photographer present. The Japanese know the power of information—frontline information.

Using frontline information is detailed in the tool called *marketing by talking around*. This tool involves training customer-contact employees to ask better marketing questions, such as "How did you hear about us? What is important to you in making your selection?" Then the company has a system to poll this information and fold it into strategic quality planning.

Marriott has its own brand of this tool built into its employees. I interviewed more than 2500 Marriott employees between 1985 and 1995. Each service group (housekeepers, front desk, concierge, food service) holds a monthly meeting to evaluate data observed from frontline employees.

This high-touch, informal tool is the least expensive and most underused tool. *Yet it is probably the most powerful.* The information is gathered in monthly reports that are studied for systems-related problems that are reviewed quarterly at higher levels. Patterns are very evident when managers look at the data collectively.

Data do not have to be statistical to be helpful in a CSS. Another client, Pan Pacific Hotels in Anaheim, applied this principle in its three years of stellar financial and customer satisfaction growth before it was sold to Disney in 1996. Jan Segers, the general manager, turned the hotel around based on his customer focus. Meetings were held daily to catch problems current guests were experiencing. Then, if possible, they were fixed that day. The traditional focus on statistically correct, random customer satisfaction measurement needs to be combined with these real-time, just-do-it measures. Remember, you grow your business one customer at a time. Steps that are useful in gathering data from the front line are provided in the tool tip section called *real-time fixes* (in chapter 10).

In sales meetings at Microsoft, we would designate some time to focus on wishes and needs that customers were raising in our contact with them. In how many sales meetings do they actually ask the sales-people what customers are saying? Then, what is done with the data? The observation section in chapter 10 covers how to roll up this data.

Ritz Carlton in the United States has adopted some of this employee involvement in order to mass customize its measurement system. Employees are trained to observe the preferences of customers and report those preferences in the database. On the next visit, a guest who prefers a feather pillow may find a feather pillow on the bed without ever knowing why.[5] The focus is on subliminally delighting customers with the ability to mass customize your service or product in the guest database—real time, every time.

Most of the high-performing companies I work with also train their customers. Companies that train their customers include Charles Schwab, Prism, Fluor Daniel, Zytec, AT&T Universal Card Services, Corning, Microsoft, and dozens of others. One heating, ventilation, and air conditioning (HVAC) company we work with trains repair-people on "house inspections." After the repairperson has completed the original fix, he or she spends 15 minutes inspecting for carbon monoxide leaks, piping problems, and other HVAC issues. This house inspection educates customers about pending problems and accounts for 30 percent of the company's downstream business. The benefit: customers who are trained to use your services or products buy more (known as *upselling*) and tend to be more satisfied.

Customer involvement is also used in many successful product launches. Sampling has been a loyalty building strategy of many grocery packaged goods and high-tech companies. How many samples of shampoo, cereal, or America Online have you received in your mailbox? Giving people samples leads about 60 percent of customers to purchase. Long-term partnerships are worth short-term losses. Toshiba gave away its digital movie player in hopes of selling disks. Computer Associates gave away its Smart Money software in hopes of selling related products and upgrades. Thus, the razor and the razor blade tactic live in high-tech.[6]

> *The new rules require more than ingenuity, agility, and speed. The value will be in establishing a long-term relationship with a customer—even if it means giving the first generation of the product away.*[7]

Thus, customer and employee involvement stretches from design and launch of the product or service to the design and launch of the CSS itself.

A Passion for Excellence

A passion for excellence resides in the heart. Hiring people with a passion for excellence is a critical ingredient for success in the increasingly competitive business world. Herb Kelleher, chief executive officer (CEO) of the highly successful Southwest Airlines, advocates hiring enthusiasm ahead of skills. He maintains that skills can be easily trained into enthusiastic people. Mike Cutchall, the chief operating officer (COO) of Prism Radio Partners, a radio broadcasting company, mentioned the same attribute when asked what he considered the most critical ingredient to success. He responded, "A passion for what you are doing." Mike was highly admired within the Prism ranks. His employees called his highly successful management style, "Mike's magic." By using a robust customer satisfaction measurement system and some of Mike's magic, the company tripled its profits and revenues in two years. How much did it cost? The CSS made money within two months of its existence.

A passion for excellence also means a passion for detail. Retail is detail. So is excellence in every other industry. Honda uses all of the standard research tools, including surveys and focus groups. It also takes videotapes of customers driving its vehicles. As a result, it has made thousands of changes in the Accord since it was introduced in 1976. Ben Knight, vice president for research and development of Honda, says:

> *We believe that the market and the customer will always find the truth.*[8]

As a result, the Honda Accord was the top-selling car between 1989 and 1992, until the Ford Taurus finally beat it out. How? An excellent video clip on *Quality Minutes* shows the level of customer needs assessment used in the design.[9] When Ford designed the Taurus, it started by having a cross-functional team identify some of the best-in-class of the 400 features that contribute to the touch and feel of a quality car. Design teams then proceeded to equal or exceed the best-in-class. This attention to detail helped to make Ford the best-selling car in the United States in the mid-1990s.

This book will focus on the common and the uncommon tools used by successful companies to know their customers. The tool master's passion for excellence is a prerequisite for a gold CSS.

Mass Customization

Advances in technology have made it possible to customize products, services, and CSSs to meet individual customer needs. Manufacturers like Matsushita and Levi Strauss are mass customizing their products (bikes and jeans respectively) to custom-fit their customers. Both companies measure customers' body dimensions and form-fit the bicycle or jeans through computer-based manufacturing.

Juki, a Japanese manufacturer of sewing machines and integrated circuit boards, said that this mass customization has actually reduced costs because of the discipline it imposes on the organization.[10] Juki has one of the most agile manufacturing plants in the world. Thirty years ago Juki needed 1000 workers to do what 12 now do.

Mass customization is also working its way into the customer satisfaction measurement system. The tools you choose need to match the type of product or service you offer. Chapter 4 on selecting tools will talk about how to match the "intimacy," or depth, of the measurement tool with the intimacy of your product or service. Intimacy, in this book, means how vital your product or service is to that person's success (professional or personal). A physician who uses a hospital facility daily has a different level of interest in improving a hospital than a one-time patient. Incentives for the latter to participate may have to be more enticing.

Methods of delivering a survey are also being mass customized. Biosym, a biomedical software branch of Corning, has its customers give feedback over electronic data interchange. Wainwright, the auto and aerospace parts manufacturer that won the Malcolm Baldrige National Quality Award in 1994, asks customers how they want to receive their monthly satisfaction survey—by mail, fax, phone, or in person. Wainwright will deliver it whichever way the customer prefers. Jo Sanders said that 95 percent of its customers wanted to receive the survey by fax.[11]

Even the questions that are asked on the surveys need to be mass customized for the various segments of your customers. Armstrong Building Products Operation, winner of the 1995 Baldrige Award, makes ceiling coverings. It found four primary segments in its customer base. When asked, each segment valued slightly different aspects of the ceiling product and services. For instance, architects' key requirements were specifications, aesthetics selection, installation, and catalogs. Residential users' key requirements focused on finished appearance and ease of installation.[12]

Real-Time, Every Time Customer Satisfaction

Whether it is high-tech computers or high-touch services, the winning way to keep in touch with customers is a real-time, dynamic model of simultaneously measuring and serving customers' needs. The model encourages companies to train employees to instantly observe a customer's needs and know how to adjust the service or product accordingly. This technique can be as simple as a hotel van driver being gregarious with a gregarious group and quiet while transporting a muted group to the hotel. The same applies for a travel agent taking an order for a ticket.

Adjusting the personality and services according to customers' needs can increase customer satisfaction. American Airlines offers expedited meal service to first-class passengers on international flights who want to eat quickly so they can either sleep or work. The traditional European-style service is available for those who want to relax. Real time, every time may also mean that the customer service person has the power to provide vouchers if the service doesn't meet expectations. Going for the gold means a paradigm shift from the old statistical and theoretical models of sampling the average customer for the satisfaction level. The new model is much more in depth, dynamic, and responsive.

A real-time, every time customer satisfaction model goes way beyond just using a written survey and taking action on it once a year. Customer needs are taken to depths of design. Koichi Nishimura, CEO of the highly successful customized manufacturing company Solectron, defined *customer-driven agile manufacturing. Agility* was defined as sustainable ability to consistently drive profit in an unpredictable world. Key words were *sustainable and consistent profit.* Solectron has hit 67 percent compounded growth over the last 17 years. Earnings per share grew just as rapidly.[13]

Nishimura cited examples of those companies that weren't agile enough to see the changes going on around them. The Swiss made better and better watches until the Japanese showed up with quartz watches. IBM got caught not noticing that distributed systems and personal computers were taking over. Cray got caught with parallel processes. Nishimura said:

> *"People want products and services faster, better and cheaper.*
>
> *They want it now. They want it where they want it, when they want it, how they want it."*

Nishimura commented that you have to be good *every* time in order to compete. You have to compete every day, for every customer. We are in a time-based economy. Nishimura should know. Solectron won the 1991 Baldrige Award, the gold medal of quality for U.S. companies.

Thus, successful companies have gone from linear measurement systems, for example, from an annual written survey to a much more dynamic, real-time measurement system. MCI and Gallup have co-developed a 24-hour polling system that provides incentives to movie-goers to call an 800 number with their instant reaction to a movie within 24 hours of seeing it so that advertising can be tweaked, increased, or aborted—depending on the reactions of the first viewers.[14] Timing on $60 million worth of advertising is critical.

Summary

Some of the current problems and opportunities in hearing the voice of the customer were covered in this chapter. The problems include surveys that provide too little wisdom, too late. Customers make their buying decisions based on how your services or products stack up against the competition. Competitor information is important. Too many companies rely on superficial measures to tap a deep understanding of high-tech, high-touch, or high-stakes services and products. Managing customer expectations happens as you are measuring them. Likewise, the price of your product must be related to the perceived customer value. The last problem is the lack of testing the tools before they were deployed.

With every set of problems comes a set of opportunities, such as ways to use your CSS to truly partner with and even delight your customers. Strategically focusing on customers who are important to your bottom line comes first. Then, focusing on the exact issues that are important to that group comes second. Asking for both customer and employee involvement in designing your CSS is also highly related to success. The passion for excellence shows through your commitment to rigor in both measurement and implementing change. Customers are quickly getting used to the increased focus on mass customization—being able to tailor the service, product, or even customer satisfaction measurement system to them. Finally, the advanced state of CSS is being able to fix problems on the spot—real time, every time. In order to do this, companies need to customize not only their research, but their products and services. The next chapter will help you set up a CSS plan so that your search for gold is easier and more successful.

Notes

1. Terence Pare, "How to Find Out What They Want," *FORTUNE* 39 (autumn/winter 1993): 39.

2. Susan B. Stoev, senior consumer research analyst, Eastman Kodak, interview with author, Washington, D.C., 20 February 1996.

3. Sheila Kessler, *Total Quality Service: A Simplified Approach to Using the Baldrige Award Criteria* (Milwaukee: ASQC Quality Press, 1995).

4. Terry McDermott, "Airlines: How Low Can They Go," *Seattle Times*, 24 April 1994, A14.

5. Christopher Hart, president, Spire Group Ltd., "Mass Customization: Pushing the Customer Satisfaction Envelope" (speech given at the 7th Annual Customer Satisfaction and Quality Measurement Conference, Dallas, Texas, 20 February 1995).

6. Neil Gross and Peter Coy, "The Technology Paradox," *Business Week*, 6 March 1995, 77.

7. Gross and Coy, "The Technology Paradox," 77.

8. Pare, "How to Find Out What They Want," 39.

9. Center for Video Education, *Quality Minutes* videotape (North White Plains, N.Y.: Center for Video Education).

10. Nakamura, manager at Juki plant, interview with author, Ohtawara, Japan, 6 October 1992.

11. Jo Sanders, customer service manager at Wainwright, interview with author, Washington, D.C., 7 February 1995.

12. Gerald L. Glenn, "Customer Focus and Satisfaction Presentation" (speech given at Quest for Excellence Conference, Washington, D.C., 8 February 1995).

13. Nishimura, speech given at Quest for Excellence Conference, Washington, D.C., 8 February 1995.

14. Jon Brecka, "The Gallup 800 Survey Customer Satisfaction Revolution," *Quality Progress* 26, no. 12 (December 1993): 16.

Going-for-the-Gold CSS: CSS Plan

Steps	Elements

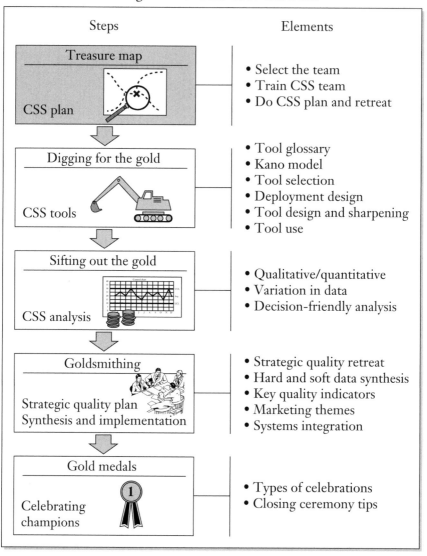

Treasure map

CSS plan

- Select the team
- Train CSS team
- Do CSS plan and retreat

Digging for the gold

CSS tools

- Tool glossary
- Kano model
- Tool selection
- Deployment design
- Tool design and sharpening
- Tool use

Sifting out the gold

CSS analysis

- Qualitative/quantitative
- Variation in data
- Decision-friendly analysis

Goldsmithing

Strategic quality plan
Synthesis and implementation

- Strategic quality retreat
- Hard and soft data synthesis
- Key quality indicators
- Marketing themes
- Systems integration

Gold medals

Celebrating
champions

- Types of celebrations
- Closing ceremony tips

Chapter 3

The Treasure Map: Designing the Customer Satisfaction System

In the gold rush for client opinions, many companies lift the pick and proclaim, "We want to do a customer survey!" The problem with that is they don't have a sense of why they are doing it, where to go for the data, or what to do once they get the data. These companies learn that they can get a lot of dirt when mining gold. Companies need to know where they are going with a good map and use reliable and speedy vehicles to get there.

The purpose of this chapter is to describe the CSS plan and planning process—the treasure map. This treasure map is vital to finding real gold instead of fool's gold. First, are you using the right tools? Second, is the tool designed well? Too many surveys ask the wrong questions of the wrong customers, at the wrong time and in the wrong way. Planning is critical.

If you are doing this planning process for the first time, you may find that it takes as long as a week for the team to do it. A major piece of this time is used to train the team. If you are more experienced, the planning process can take as little as two days. After you have your plan in place, it is fairly easy to revise and maintain it.

The steps in designing the CSS plan are as follows:

- Select your CSS steering committee and leader.
- Introduce the CSS steering committee to the CSS plan development process
- Have the CSS retreat(s)
- Hire or select a CSS research director
- Consider other examples of gold CSSs

Select Your CSS Steering Committee and Leader

Measuring and managing customer satisfaction is best orchestrated by a team, with an individual as the key owner. An executive sponsor is critical because change is so difficult. Customer needs assessment and satisfaction results usually require product, service, systems, or policy *change*. Without the clout and representation a well-selected team brings, implementation of desired change will be more difficult.

If you don't have an executive sponsor or some sort of high-level committee overseeing this process, that will be your first step. You will need to do some selling first. One of the best ways is to bring someone in from the outside who can tie customer satisfaction to financial success. Half- or full-day executive seminars are invaluable in getting executives' attention and helping them go down the right track. The right track includes seeing how critical the CSS is to their financial success, making sure the right people are selected for the CSS steering committee, and seeing that adequate resources are provided to make a CSS plan worthwhile.

Most executives have not had customer satisfaction experience as part of their earlier career or education. Life wasn't so fiercely competitive in the 1950s–1980s. Suggest that your executive(s) go to the high-status Quest for Excellence Conference, held every February in Washington, D.C. At the conference the Baldrige Award–winning companies describe how they achieved their best-in-class performance. The level of sophistication of customer satisfaction measurement systems in these successful companies is usually an eye-opener. ASQC will provide more information (call toll free, 800-248-1946). ASQC also offers courses on customer retention and survey design.

The following criteria are helpful when selecting your gold diggers. You need

- People who are respected for their customer service and successes
- Personalities that can help sell the system and resources needed
- Representatives from various departments
- Representatives from various levels (executive to front line)

This list stems from trying many other different selection criteria and seeing what doesn't work. If the level is all from the executive rank, then the frontline nuances are lost. If the level is all middle management, power struggles and positioning tend to be prominent. If just one department is represented, then the questions tend to be skewed in that direction. Thus, a diagonal slice of the organization is your best bet.

Functions from which to draw the group include sales, customer service, quality, manufacturing or operations, finance, and product/service development. If the group exceeds about 10 members, decision making bogs down. If you are part of a large organization, you might try using advisors to feed your group. Bring them in for certain pieces of your agenda, but do not make them a central part of the decision making.

One of the considerations is usually whether to bring in the union. Even though obstacles can be formidable, the frontline workers will be the ones who implement change. Having unions represented on the CSS steering committee says a lot for the respect management shows the employees who "make it happen." Armstrong Building Products Division, a highly successful winner of the 1995 Baldrige Award, has union representation on its executive committee.

Again, picking personalities, levels, and various functions is one of the trickiest parts of a successful measuring and managing effort. One successful method is to stipulate the criteria for selection (team player, customer focused, well-respected, high standards) and have people vote on who could best represent them. Make sure that at least one or two well-respected, risk-taking executive sponsors are part of the CSS steering committee. If the CSS steering committee is a separate group from the executive team (it usually is), the two need to be closely linked. Each set of decisions from the CSS steering committee needs approval from the executive team. The one or two executive sponsors should sit in on both meetings.

Introduce the CSS Steering Committee to the CSS Plan Development Process

In an introductory meeting the facilitator explains both the two-phase planning process and the approximate schedule for plan development. The individuals in the group are introduced and the reasons why they were chosen (or nominated) are given.

Homework and deadlines also need to be given for securing the following information prior to the phase I retreat.

- Market segments by products and by types of customers.
- Revenues, profits, growth, and market share of each segment.
- Company strategy for penetrating each strategy.
- Review of what CSS tools and systems are currently in place. That includes the reports from each one of the tools.

An experienced CSS facilitator is needed to prepare for the CSS retreat. If you don't have a qualified candidate on the inside, you might consider having an internal understudy to take over during subsequent rounds. The facilitator then integrates the information prior to the first meeting and determines the best way to focus the CSS efforts.

The CSS steering committee also needs to do some homework prior to the first meeting. In addition to reading this book, committee members might consider reading the following books:

- *Managing Customer Value* by Bradley T. Gale[1]
- *Customer Satisfaction Measurement and Management* by Earl Naumann and Kathleen Giel[2]

I typically divide the CSS retreat into two different meetings. The length of each meeting is also indicated.

- CSS conceptual design—three to four days
- CSS final plan—two to three days

The length of the two meetings can be divided in half if the company or unit has fewer than 300 people. Elements can also be eliminated, depending on the experience and sophistication of the current system and people. This two-phase process, which combines training the CSS steering committee and working on the plan, has worked well for all kinds of industries—fast food, engineering, broadcasting, insurance, customized manufacturing, distribution, electronics, software, government agencies, utilities, energy, airlines, hotels, and others.

Have the CSS Retreat(s)

As was mentioned earlier, the CSS planning retreat usually unfolds in two separate meetings, with preparation and implementation happening between each meeting. It is important that these meetings be held off-site so that quality attention can be given to each element. Phase I and II retreats are to develop and finalize the plan. Exhibit 3.1 shows phase I, the CSS conceptual design retreat. This is just a sample and is usually modified based on where the organization is in its evolution. Systems issues include who will own what data, how accountability will be built into the system, communication of results, training, executive involvement, making the CSS a positive rather than a negative experience, and so on.

The CSS steering committee then has homework to do on double-checking figures, seeking additional information it needs to develop, checking out available resources to use for implementation, and having others review this conceptual CSS plan. An initial customer telephone survey may also happen after this first session to determine which factors customers want you to track and how they would like you to track them. Various segments of your customer base may have various preferences.

The initial tools are usually launched after phase II training (see Exhibit 3.2). Usually coaching and monitoring the data gatherers is required in the first round of using the instruments. Selection of

---

- The importance of integrating customer, quality, financial, and employee data
- The importance of a multipoint listening-post system
- How to set the mission and objectives for the CSS plan
- How to segment the customers and set priorities on who to measure
- How to make the tools scientific and systematic
- What tools serve what functions
- How to match tools to those objectives
- How to choose the right questions to ask
- How to design the questions, format, and scaling on the questionnaire
- How to increase the response rate on the selected tools
- What software or hardware can help gather and analyze data
- What systems need to be put into place to make a CSS plan work

Exhibit 3.1   Agenda for the phase I conceptual design retreat.

- CSS conceptual plan modifications according to the feedback
- Customer priorities review
- Tool refinement to meet customer needs in tracking
- Question refinement to check for bias, ambiguity, scaling, etc.
- Data gathering devices and automation (computers, software, etc.)
- Project plan: goals, schedule, cost, roles, resources needed
- Communication plan: to managers, employees, and customers
- Integration plan: how to scale questions so they can be rolled-up
- CSS improvement plan: how the system will be improved

Exhibit 3.2   Agenda for the phase II CCS plan finalizing retreat.

telephone interviewers is critical if the survey will be done by phone. Training and monitoring the interviewers may also be necessary.

Specific Ideas for the Phase I Retreat

Determine Your Mission, Objectives and Level of Commitment. The starting place is your company mission. Check to see that your CSS mission ties into your overall company mission. For instance, at Prism Radio Partners the mission was:

> *To develop and implement a Prism-wide customer satisfaction measurement system that will enable us to continuously improve our quality of service while exceeding the expectations of our clients.*

We would start subsequent meetings with this mission. This focus on the mission kept us from getting lost in the details.

After you have decided on your tools, you also might want to complete a checklist for success (see Exhibit 3.3). At Prism we developed a list of success criteria against which our tools would be evaluated.

Ideas for benefits were also brainstormed and listed in Exhibit 3.4. Each member of the CSS steering committee knew it was his or her

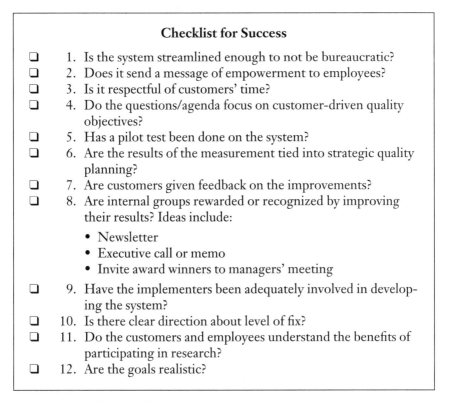

Checklist for Success

❏   1. Is the system streamlined enough to not be bureaucratic?
❏   2. Does it send a message of empowerment to employees?
❏   3. Is it respectful of customers' time?
❏   4. Do the questions/agenda focus on customer-driven quality objectives?
❏   5. Has a pilot test been done on the system?
❏   6. Are the results of the measurement tied into strategic quality planning?
❏   7. Are customers given feedback on the improvements?
❏   8. Are internal groups rewarded or recognized by improving their results? Ideas include:

   • Newsletter
   • Executive call or memo
   • Invite award winners to managers' meeting

❏   9. Have the implementers been adequately involved in developing the system?
❏   10. Is there clear direction about level of fix?
❏   11. Do the customers and employees understand the benefits of participating in research?
❏   12. Are the goals realistic?

Exhibit 3.3   Checklist for success.

responsibility to sell the concept of a gold CSS plan into the departments, divisions, or units. We also developed a sales kit consisting of transparencies, a fact sheet, and bulletin-board materials for each of the CSS steering committee members to use.

In addition, you need to decide the executive-level commitment to customer focus. Being honest can be tough. Sometimes senior managers say they want to hear from customers, but when the customer says, "We need a three-day turnaround in your billing process," the reaction is, "We can't possibly do that." Achieving three days may take an investment in a more modern billing system and more training. When these conflicts arise between the status quo and customers' needs, information about competitors is usually helpful. Many times the customers have been exposed to a better way and are considering shifting. Benchmarking (looking at what others are doing in that area) can help managers realize that they need to speed up their change process.

Customers:
      Get better service, products, and results
      Heighten sense of partnership and relationship
      Tangible incentives
      Learn about a gold CSS to be applied in their business
Sales:
      Increase revenues through upselling satisfied customers
      Reduce attrition
      Improve sales skills
      Improve marketing focus and relationships
      Position company to attract new business
      Reflect high standards of company
      Enhance sense of pride with leading-edge company
Employees:
      Recognition and rewards given to successes
      Increased ownership of customer satisfaction issues
      Increased creativity in problem resolution
      Good resume builder
Managers and executives:
      Be able to manage budget according to priorities
      Provide input on training and systems issues
      Help focus on customer-driven recognition and reward for
         successes
      Can recruit better people

Exhibit 3.4   Positive benefits of a gold CSS.

Do you include questions about issues when you know you won't change? You need to ask this when determining the issues that are important for customers to have you track. If you don't ask about pricing issues and that is your customers' key buying criterion, you will find yourself left in the dust by competitors who are asking about and focusing on what is important. On the other hand, if you find that prices are important to your customers and still decide that you will not entertain changes in reducing your costs, then don't ask details about pricing preferences on your satisfaction measures. Asking questions that customers know is a dissatisfier and then making no changes is very frustrating to customers and will cause them to drop out of your CSS query. Have your executives review the questions and see if there are any questions with topics that are nonnegotiable. Having executives and managers buy in to the questions that are asked helps with their acceptance of the data.

> *A gold CSS mind-set is open to changing any dissatisfiers that are deemed important to key customers.*

Understanding the Science of the System and Tools. *Scientific* means that you are rigorous about how you gather and use your data. One CEO of an failing apparel store with more than 300 outlets was asked how he researched the needs of his customers. He said he had a scientific process. Once a year he visited several stores as a mystery shopper and talked to several employees. From that tiny sampling (of employees rather than customers) he made strategic decisions about customers' clothing preferences and their view of the sales experience. Making strategic decisions about the direction of the company on a tiny response rate of a tiny sample size is scary.

The reason why surveys contain quantitative measurements is so you can compare data. Without being able to make meaningful comparisons to how you did in previous years or how you did against your competition, you are limiting the usefulness of the data. The key elements of being scientific are sampling, reliability, and validity. This book only provides a basic understanding of these statistical concepts. If you want highly statistically reliable and valid surveys, as mentioned before, I recommend Bob E. Hayes' book, *Measuring Customer Satisfaction*.[3]

In addition to being rigorous about the science, make sure you don't become seduced into the black hole of statistical accuracy. My own experience concurs with the Japanese. They think there are two extremes in this country: overly scientific or overly intuitive. Overly scientific means that our planning offices are deluged with highly scientific data that doesn't translate into action. The measures are so precise that they don't really capture what customers care about. Talking to customers when, where, and how they want to give feedback and then rolling-up the information is important in companies that are passionate about measuring *and managing* customer satisfaction.

Overly intuitive means few customer satisfaction measures exist at all. If a survey does exist, it has been casually constructed and deployed. Management thus relies on intuition to make decisions.

Qualitative information can be managed and integrated into scores to provide a deeper understanding of why the numbers are what they are.

The Japanese are more likely to do their surveying by observing rigorously, gathering extensive field data from dealers and retailers, reviewing hard data, taking pictures of how people are using their products or services, and then setting strategic quality objectives by synthesizing that data. One highly scientific customer satisfaction survey just doesn't work for a real-time, every time system. It is just too slow and too superficial.

Going for the gold focuses on timing, so that your measurement system allows you to be competitive. Being competitive in the next millennium means being able to respond quickly and efficiently. In order to do that, some science is sacrificed. Reliability is important, for instance. You want to make sure that customers don't fill out the survey based on a meeting they just had, feeling ill that day, or not understanding the questions. Repeating questions is one way to check for reliability. But low-relationship customers don't return long surveys with repeat questions. Thus, you have trade-offs between getting more reliability (asking repeat questions) and ending up with an irritating, longer survey or sacrificing some reliability for a higher response rate and less customer irritation.

Thus, the advice in this section is based on being both scientific and practical. The tips will help you increase reliability and be able to predict revenues and profits without being overly cumbersome.

> *It is better to have a good multiple measurement system that retains and delights customers than it is to have a highly scientific survey that drives customers away.*

On the other hand, don't base conclusions on too few gold customers that represent a vocal but unrepresentative minority. You then turn off the many to please the few. Rigorous random sampling is necessary if you don't sample 100 percent.

Systematic means that you use your tools at regular intervals. Systematic means that you use the feedback to drive your strategic quality goals; that you have regular procedures, processes, and standards in measurement.

Segment Your Customers and Focus on the Mother Lode: Target Customers and Their Concerns.   Linking your customer satisfaction system to your financial success starts with a focus on your high-profit and high-growth customers. Thus, segmenting your customers into cells can help you determine which segments to highlight.

Why bother with segmentation? Most companies want to know what differences exist in different regions (parts of the town or country, different product lines, or major types of customers). CompUSA has home office users, pleasure users, and major business accounts. It needs to know how needs differ for both marketing and reengineering purposes. United Van Lines has government, residential, and commercial accounts. Government accounts are the least profitable, while residential accounts have the highest cost of sales. Commercial customers therefore may be its gold. An orthodontist might have children, adults, and parents as patients—all with different sets of needs and different priorities. One very successful temporary employment agency has at least two different sets of satisfaction questions after learning that construction clients and administrative clients had different needs they wanted to track. Not only do you need to look at customizing your system and questions according to segments, but you also need to set priorities about which segments you need to tackle first and spend the most money on. Mass customization is the wave of the future.

Gold customers should be taken more seriously than the others. Why? The old Vilfredo Pareto rule applies—most businesses receive 80 percent of their revenues from just 20 percent of their customers. More than 60 percent of Delta's revenues come from just 6 percent of its customer base. Each business may have a segment that is low profit, high frustration. My chimney sweep gave me excellent advice years ago. He said "You know, 20 percent of my customers accounted for 80 percent of my frustration. They were very demanding without giving me much in return. The best thing I did was drop those clients." National Car Rental now has customers fill out a "Good Driver Analysis." If the renter is a high risk, he or she cannot rent a car. Insurance costs are way down, and internal administrative systems have been streamlined as a result. Why spend 80 percent of your energy on 20 percent of your customers? Just say no.

In our research with engineering, broadcast, transportation, engineering, and other high-partnership companies, we found that less equals more. Surprisingly, we found a correlation between the highest revenue, market share, and profit units of different companies and the brevity of their customer list. Having too small a list is usually dangerous, but focusing at the right end of the spectrum has helped these companies spend more time on target customers.

Many companies get caught up in trying to please every element of their client base while neglecting their gold clients. Success is going to be related to a company's discipline in attending to the highest potential of employees and customers. Thus, the moral of the story is:

> *Spend your greatest energy on mining solid gold clients.*

Note this approach to customer satisfaction research is a radical departure from the traditional homogenous look at the average customer. Technology has allowed us to ask, "Who are the customers most important to us, and what do they contribute to profit?" Technology allows us to use the information that links the financial investment a company makes in a particular customer and the return that customer generates to the company.[4]

You don't need to be a large company to use this segmentation. Prism, like most radio broadcasting companies, has two sets of customers, listeners and advertisers. The programming group was doing extensive research on the music mix most desirable to their listening audience. Ratings are critical to the success of a radio station. Pleasing the listeners pleases the advertisers, who buy time.

With this listener research already working well, we chose to focus on the advertisers. As with most companies, we found that 80 percent of the revenues came from roughly 20 percent of the customer base. Because we didn't have the budget to do a quality job with all of the advertiser base, we chose to focus on the gold advertisers—those in the top 20 percent revenue tier. That allowed us to do telephone surveys rather than written ones, institute advisory groups, and do special research projects on that group.

Segmenting your customer base will vary, depending on your product or service. Another example is a software client that found that its pharmaceutical segment represented 64 percent of its overall profit (see Exhibit 3.5). Thus, it chose to focus on that segment of the company's business.

Another major telecommunications client chose to segment using size of phone system. First it separated its business into large, medium and small phone systems, based on the number of incoming lines. It took the gold customers (top 20 percent in profit contributions) of the large and medium systems groups. That allowed the company to do more in-depth research with fewer numbers of more profitable cus-

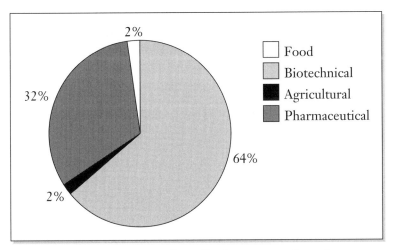

Exhibit 3.5   Software company: Contributions to overall profit.

tomers. Previously, the focus had been on the whole customer pool, with every customer getting an equal vote. When using traditional segmentation, consider these elements.

- Are the cells (divisions) large enough to give you statistically usable data?
- Are the segments in line with your organization?
- Are the segments separate and distinct?
- Do you need that level of segmentation?

An example of what can happen if you don't do this segmentation is evidenced by Delta Airlines. When all the airlines were revamping their frequent flyer programs in the mid-1990s to be more cost-effective, Delta did the same. Delta researched its customers and gave everyone an equal vote. Delta concluded it would be competitive by offering a free ticket with 25,000 points rather than the previous 30,000 points. Sounds great! It was great for the less-profitable customers, the discounted-ticket leisure segment. But the frequent flyers in the Platinum program were irritated. The old program allowed Platinum members to get a free ticket after 20,000 points. The new program equalized the low- and high-usage travelers into one lump and required 25,000 points for everyone. Since 60 percent of Delta's profits come from 6 percent of the customers, this was the wrong group to irritate.

Yet Delta had *targeted* business and international customers as its strategic markets. Delta listened to the complaints from the highly profitable members of its business advisory board and made concessions to appease the upset group. It changed the program so that old points could be redeemed with old requirements for the Platinum group. The result: a complicated system that is difficult for everyone (including the employees) to understand. At least Delta listened to the complaints.

One technique you might use in this segmentation exercise is called *hot cells*. Segment your customer base using a grid that looks like Exhibit 3.6. Then find a cell that is either your highest profit, highest revenues, or highest growth and focus on that hot cell for your initial research efforts. When you have accomplished that research, then move onto the next highest priority cell. Exhibit 3.6 lists the market segments in the left column and then divides each of those segments into geographical territories. The cells then reflect last year's growth rate in terms of overall contribution to profit. You can see that the highest growth cells are the Pacific Rim and European pharmaceutical companies. You might choose to focus on these two cells first. Then you would move to the biotech companies on the west coast that are also showing profound growth.

The statistical process of sampling here is called *stratified random sampling*. You have stratified your customer base. If a segment has suddenly slipped when the competitors' shares have risen, this too might be a segment to target for in-depth understanding.

If Delta had stratified its customer base for its customer needs assessment, it would not have proclaimed to the Platinum members

Market/segment	Percent revenue	Eastern U.S. revenue	Western U.S. revenue	Pacific Rim revenue	European revenue
Pharmaceuticals	64%	Down 15%	Up 7%	Up 56%	Up 45%
Biotech	32%	Flat	Up 75%	Flat	Up 25%
Agriculture	2%				
Food	2%				

Exhibit 3.6   Hot cells in revenue growth.

that the new program was "based on research of our customers." While the statement is true, the methodology needs improvement for a profit-driven company that doesn't want to irritate its key customers with its research practices.

Keep in mind that *you don't have to sample all of your customers.* If you have limited funds, focus on your high-profit or high-growth customer segments. That may mean telephone surveys instead of written surveys for that group. It may mean a larger sample size from the high end strata than from the low end. It may mean more tools are used to assess the high end than the low end. Delta self-corrected because the business advisory board and complaint tracking helped it realize the difficulty with its initial research. That is part of the benefit of having diverse tools so that you don't count on just one point of input.

Understand that each research contact you have with your customers communicates that you care about them (if you do a good job). Just reaching out and touching your high-end customers not only measures their reactions, but also cements your relationship further. They feel more a part of your company. Delta couldn't have a more loyal group of advocates than the people on those business advisory boards. That alone is worth the expense of going deeper. Each of those advisory board members easily had a lifetime worth to Delta of $1 million to billions of dollars.

> *It costs five to seven times more to recruit a new customer as it does to retain one.*[5]

Eventually your customer satisfaction measurement and management system can be tailored to each important customer instead of segments. The questions may differ. At this real-time, every time point, you will have delegated much of the measurement and management down to the local level with a trained, standardized way of measuring customers. That allows for lower-cost local contact and higher-order roll-up of data.

Most Fortune 1000 companies we work with are at the early stages of this downward empowerment with the CSS. Deploying the measures at the frontline level requires considerable investment in training and monitoring. Companies first have to coordinate at the top and learn how to use multifaceted tools wisely. Then they can cascade the process downward, train at the local level, and count on consistent data collection, analysis, and roll-up from a local level. It is much like building an accounting system that uses the same software, analysis, and reporting structure, but is managed and maintained by accountants or bookkeepers at the local level. The flow of CSS design, implementation, and fixes through to the inner fiber of the organization is where the three happy faces reside.

Marriott is close to this real-time, every time measurement and management level. Consistency of high standards is evident across its 100,000-plus employees. Marriott has also focused on creating a welcome environment for employees so that employees can extend themselves to customers. Marriott, like most high-performing service companies, has also focused on hiring the right personalities to pre-load their system with good people.

Specifics on the Project Plan: Who, What, Where, How Many, How. Before you do the project plan, read the next chapter and choose the tools. The project plan will merely detail who will do what to whom and by when. Exhibit 3.7 displays a sample project plan tool table.

Exhibit 3.8 shows a Gantt chart with a year-long schedule. A longer term schedule might also be helpful. The mission, project plan table, and Gantt chart make it easy to communicate your intentions to internal and external customers.

What tool	Objective	Sample	Owner	By when	Comments
Focus groups	Find what is important	8 groups of key customers	Person X QIT* X	6/1	
Telephone survey	Satisfaction measure	80% of the gold 40% of the rest	Person Y QIT Y	10/1	
Lost customers	Find out why customers are leaving	80% of the gold 20% of the rest	Person Z QIT Z	12/1	
Etc. etc.					
* QIT = Quality improvement team					

Exhibit 3.7   Sample project plan tool table.

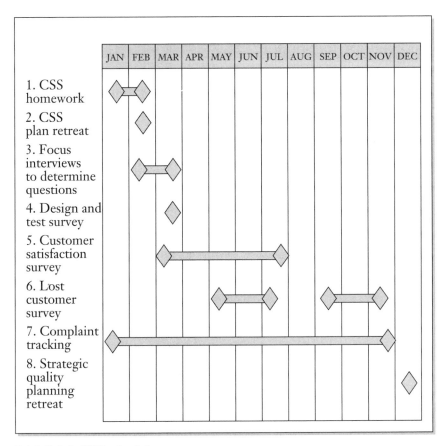

	JAN	FEB	MAR	APR	MAY	JUN	JUL	AUG	SEP	OCT	NOV	DEC
1. CSS homework	◇—◇											
2. CSS plan retreat		◇										
3. Focus interviews to determine questions		◇—◇										
4. Design and test survey			◇									
5. Customer satisfaction survey			◇——————◇									
6. Lost customer survey					◇—◇				◇—◇			
7. Complaint tracking	◇——————————————————◇											
8. Strategic quality planning retreat											◇	

Exhibit 3.8 CSS schedule.

Match the Tools to Your Customers' Level of Use and Sophistication. The point is not to use all of the CSS tools, but to carefully select those tools that will help your company deliver services or products better, cheaper, and faster. The next chapter will help you design an easy-to-use, cost-effective system with the right mix of tools. You will need to choose a few good tools that are appropriate to your particular company's type of service and product, your objectives, and your commitment to the process.

Products or services involve varying degrees of relationships with customers. High-relationship products or services are either high touch, high stake, high ticket, or high tech. *High touch* means the customer has lots of contact with people in the organization; hotels, air-lines, and restaurants are examples. *High stakes* mean that the service or product is vital to the customers' success; a biomedical software program may be critical to the success of a biomedical researcher. *High tech* means that the technology is complicated and the customer needs to be educated to use it properly. High-ticket products or ser-vices (more than $100) have more money at risk, so people may be more cautious.

With high-relationship products or services, be more personal in your choice of tools and use those tools more frequently. Instead of doing written customer satisfaction surveys, give preference to doing them by phone. The measurement system should augment relation-ships. Most written surveys are good for report cards but don't allow penetrating below the surface. Exhibit 3.9 shows the relationship between high tech, high touch, high ticket, and high stakes to the various types of tools. The personal measures are used to develop and refine high-tech, high-touch, and high-stakes services or prod-

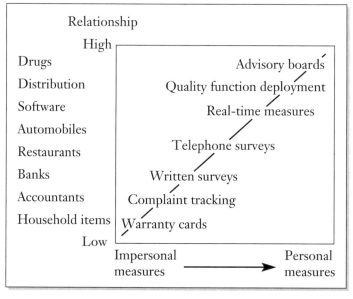

Exhibit 3.9   Choose your tools wisely.

ucts. Less-personal measures can be used for the lower end of this continuum. Exhibit 3.9 is meant to stress the emphasis on the type of tools and where your money is spent.

Note that companies within the same industry can differ. A software company like Microsoft that makes packaged software for the masses might use a system that looks very different from another software manufacturer. Microsoft does conduct a telephone survey to determine why people chose Microsoft and how they would compare Microsoft Word to Word Perfect, for instance. Biosym, on the other hand, customizes software for scientists who develop biochemical models. These scientists lease the product from Biosym. The purchase cycle for Biosym is more than a year. Training is intensive, and customers rarely switch unless they are highly dissatisfied. Microsoft needs to know more about the decision process at the point of purchase. Biosym needs to know more about how to partner with its loyal customers who lease the product from them to anticipate their ever-changing scientific needs. Microsoft uses telephone surveys and user groups as its centerpiece of customer satisfaction research. Biosym uses a much more intimate customer satisfaction system. Biosym clients frequently work with Biosym side-by-side to co-develop the product.

Thus, the rule of thumb in designing a system is:

> *High-relationship services or products need personal measurement tools.*
>
> *Low-relationship services or products can use impersonal tools.*

One company revealed an amazing phenomenon when it started making phone calls to ask about perceived quality. U.S. West found that just asking people what they thought convinced them that U.S. West was improving in these areas, "even though U.S. West hadn't made any changes." The customers queried had a 20 percent increase in quality ratings compared to those customers who hadn't been called. The perception even transferred to customers' perceptions of the quality of the transmission, "You people have sure improved the quality of your network lately. I used to get a lot of static. But now there are no mistakes."[6]

Hire or Select a CSS Research Director

An individual needs to orchestrate the tools. If the company is small (less than 300 people), one research director organizing and doing the work will probably suffice. Hiring the right person is often difficult. The individual needs the background and discipline to be well-organized, do probabilistic research sampling, and yet be able to do counseling on the phone with heated customers during complaints and lost customer satisfaction research. Likewise, the researcher needs to be respected by the managers and executives who are going to implement changes. This job description usually takes a bit of finesse. I will usually help the company with interviews so they can make the right choice. Putting the applicants through a structured role play will tell you a great amount, if you know what to look for. References are also imperative. Look for a good listener, a well-organized person who picks up on information quickly.

Consider Other Examples of Gold CSSs

North Island Federal Credit Union

Let's take an example of a credit union, a high-relationship organization. The North Island Federal Credit Union in San Diego, California won the silver level for the California Quality Award in 1994. It originally used focus groups to identify what was important to its target customers. Then it developed eight satisfiers that were the anchor of the strategic quality plan.

It currently uses an outside consulting firm at regular intervals to do surveys on these eight satisfiers. In addition, it uses debriefings with customers to determine transaction satisfaction. The credit union is only 300 people strong, but sets a stellar example of building a bridge to customers. It is currently the largest local financial institution in San Diego. Its services are a delight to customers. It is a high-relationship service.

Zytec

On the other hand, Zytec, the winner of the 1991 Baldrige Award, makes power supply equipment for computers and photocopy machines. It is a commodity and yet Zytec does considerable engineering to customize its product. It uses an outside consulting company to survey customers with a written benchmark survey that compares Zytec with competitors. Executives also have monthly quotas of customer calls that they make and ask three simple questions: (1) How are we doing on quality? (2) How is our service? (3) How is the value of our product? All of these data are reviewed at regular intervals. Zytec is a medium-relationship company.

Prism Radio Partners

A closer look at Prism Radio Partner's CSS may help you understand how it tripled its market value in three years. The research director, Marci Joyce, does all the telephone lost customer surveys, customer satisfaction surveys, perceptuals, employee exit interviews, and customer and employee attrition rates. First, Marci started with a telephone survey of lost customers. Lost customer research is done as advertisers are reported (on a monthly basis) lost by the 16 radio stations. In one year, the lost customer survey tool had recovered more than a half-million dollars in business (out of $6.7 million in profit).

The customer satisfaction telephone interviews are done once a year for all five cities. The customer satisfaction data are correlated to incremental margins, customer attrition, location profitability, and revenues. Customer attrition is also correlated to employee attrition (very highly correlated). All of the financial, quality, employee, and customer data are integrated in the yearly strategic quality planning meeting. Out of that meeting comes the handful of strategic quality initiatives for Prism. Marketing strengths are also pinpointed.

Summary

This chapter covered how the treasure map or CSS plan can help you chart your course. You need the right team at the top. Selecting and training a CSS team is the starting point. Then team members need a retereat to plan the entire CSS system. Ingredients to the plan include the mission, objectives, and criteria for success for the CSS. After the team members have been trained on what the tools can and can't do for them, they need to select the appropriate tools. Then they need to assign who will do what to whom by when—the project plan. The next chapter will detail the tools more explicitly, especially the key tools. Additional tools are provided in the tool tip section.

Notes

1. Bradley T. Gale, *Managing Customer Value* (New York: Free Press, 1994).

2. Earl Naumann and Kathleen Giel, *Customer Satisfaction Measurement and Management* (Cincinnati, Ohio: International Thomson Publishing, 1995).

3. Bob E. Hayes, *Measuring Customer Satisfaction: Development and Use of Questionnaires* (Milwaukee: ASQC Quality Press, 1992).

4. B. G. Yovovich, "High-Tech Tools Build New Concept of Market: More Sophisticated Look at Customer Emerges Via Data," *Advertising Age*, 15 October 1995, 25.

5. Frederick F. Reichheld and W. Earl Sasser Jr., "Zero Defections: Quality Comes to Service," *Harvard Business Review* (September-October 1990): 107.

6. George R. Walther, *Upside Down Marketing* (New York: McGraw-Hill, 1994).

Part II

Selection and Use of Tools

Going-for-the-Gold CSS: CSS Tools

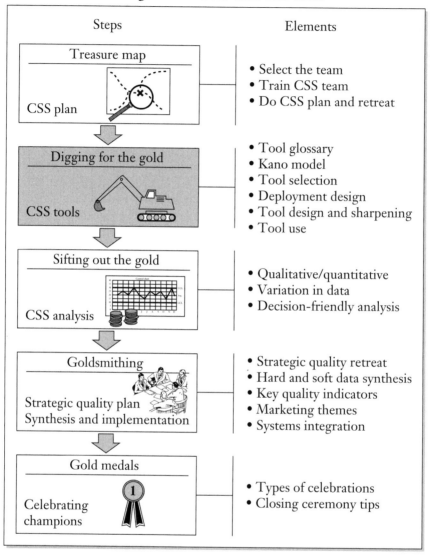

Steps	Elements
Treasure map / CSS plan	• Select the team • Train CSS team • Do CSS plan and retreat
Digging for the gold / CSS tools	• Tool glossary • Kano model • Tool selection • Deployment design • Tool design and sharpening • Tool use
Sifting out the gold / CSS analysis	• Qualitative/quantitative • Variation in data • Decision-friendly analysis
Goldsmithing / Strategic quality plan / Synthesis and implementation	• Strategic quality retreat • Hard and soft data synthesis • Key quality indicators • Marketing themes • Systems integration
Gold medals / Celebrating champions	• Types of celebrations • Closing ceremony tips

Chapter 4

Selecting Your Tools

The key steps in efficient and effective digging for gold include using the right tools and using them right. The steps on this path are as follows:

- Understand your choice of tools
- Determine where these tools fit in Kano's model of satisfaction
- Select the tools that best fit your objectives

Thus, the first step will be to define the tools. The next sections walk you through these steps.

Understand Your Choice of Tools

A glossary of customer satisfaction measurement tools is found near the end of the book. Even though you may be familiar with the tool names, you should review the definitions so that you know how the tool is discussed in the rest of this book. I have found that tool names are used interchangeably in many companies. For instance, customer satisfaction surveys are easily mixed up with perceptual surveys.

Determine Where These Tools Fit in Kano's Model of Satisfaction

Noriaki Kano described three levels of customer satisfaction: expected quality, desired quality, and excited quality. *Expected quality* measures can make or break decisions in buying. If you meet the standard, doing a better job at that feature doesn't buy more business. For example, hotel guests expect certain things in their visit. The size of a blanket on a hotel bed illustrates expected quality. If the blanket tucks under the mattress, this feature is covered. Adding more square inches may be more of a nuisance than a gain and doesn't add to satisfaction. However, the time spent waiting to check in may fall under the *desired quality* category. You would rather wait in line three minutes than 30. The shorter the wait, the greater the satisfaction. The better you are at providing desired features, the greater the satisfaction.

The third level is *excited quality*. Customers aren't expecting these features of your product or service. They are "wowed" or pleasantly surprised. Receiving champagne while you wait to check in to the hotel may be a wow experience. Note that it doesn't take long for wows to turn into expected quality, especially in these fast-moving times. Turn signals on cars were once a wow. Chocolates on the hotel room pillow were once a wow.

Exhibit 4.1 demonstrates how expected quality gives a base threshold of satisfaction. Desired quality improves satisfaction as you improve that feature. Excited quality delights.

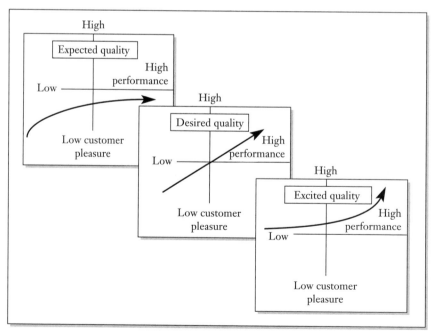

Exhibit 4.1   Kano's model: Three levels of satisfaction.

Expected and desired quality tools are reactive. They tend to catch what customers consider as basic to staying with the company. Excited quality tools are proactive. Excited quality tools are meant to induce customer satisfaction rather than measure it. Tools can be categorized loosely into these three areas of satisfaction.

Expected quality tools

- Complaint systems
- Internal quality process measures (not discussed in this book)
- Lost customer surveys
- Attrition analysis—customer and employee
- Win/loss reports

Desired quality tools

- Customer satisfaction surveys (includes just your customers)
- Perceptual surveys (includes your competitors' customers)
- Transaction reports
- Focus interviews or groups

Excited quality tools

- Invent-the-future focus groups
- Customer loyalty programs
- Joined-at-the-hip programs
- Advisory groups

Expected tools can help you prevent defection. Customers who have left will tell you why they opted out. Complaint tracking can give you early warnings signals about the features of your service or product that cause defection. Asking customers why they chose a competitor over you also provides answers about expected levels of quality.

The main tools for desired quality are customer satisfaction surveys, perceptual surveys, and transaction surveys. Customer surveys allow you to look at trends in data. Transaction surveys allow more real-time fixes since they happen at the point of the transaction. Fixing problems in real time can mean higher satisfaction scores on the overall customer satisfaction survey.

Select the Tools That Best Fit Your Objectives

Kano's model moves from a reactive to proactive approach. If you are concerned about loss of customers and getting your basic systems in place, start by focusing on the expected quality tools. If you are well beyond that, concentrate on desired and excited quality tools. Understand that a going-for-a-gold CSS starts with setting realistic objectives. It is better to select one or two tools and use them well than to select the whole smorgasbord and use them all poorly.

One hint: If you are in financial distress or are very financially focused, start with a lost customer survey. If used well, this tool provides nearly immediate return on your investment.

Likewise, the priority tools need to fit how your business operates and your customer's buying cycles. A waste management company that has two- to five-year contracts with municipalities may find that lost customers happen in the middle of projects, not at the end. If they waited until lost customer research was done at the next bid cycle, they would find the recovery rate low. In the middle of a project, the relationship can be improved. After a municipality has blackballed its waste management company, it takes years and sometimes decades to recover. Complaint management systems and customer satisfaction measures may be more critical to success for larger contracts and longer buying cycle companies.

Summary

The chapter began by stressing the importance of defining CSS tools. Kano's model of satisfaction helps divide the tools into two categories: reactive and proactive. Selecting the appropriate tools means adjusting your level of depth to the level of technology, stakes, and customer contact you have. Phone surveys rather than written surveys are recommended for high-relationship services or products.

Chapter 5

Sharpening Your Tools

This chapter will first cover the key expected quality tools: complaint systems, lost customer surveys, and customer attrition analysis. The second part of this chapter will help you sharpen the customer satisfaction survey as the primary desired quality tool. Note that each of these tools has more detailed information provided in the tool tip section. The chapter concludes with some examples of excited quality tools. This chapter will help you understand the purpose of each tool in the conceptual design of the CSS plan.

Expected Quality Tools

Complaint Handling, Tracking, and Resolution Systems

Unhappy shoppers do not always express their dissatisfaction directly. At any time, 25 percent of customers are dissatisfied—but only 4 percent complain.[1] Many customers would rather switch suppliers than complain. Even more, it doesn't take much to cause a customer to switch. Forum research found that 68 percent of customers defect because of a single worker's indifference. Only 14 percent switch because of product dissatisfaction.[2]

The Technical Assistance Research Program (TARP) did extensive research on complaints throughout the 1980s and 1990s. Its research findings are as follows:[3]

- 96 percent of unhappy customers never complain.

- 68 percent of customers defect because of indifference.
- 17 percent of dissatisfied complainers will buy again.
- 73 percent of satisfied complainers will buy again.
- 8 percent to 10 percent of people hear about each complaint from the dissatisfied customer.

The benefits of a good customer complaint handling system are self-evident. More than 73 percent of satisfied complainers buy again. Only 17 percent of dissatisfied complainers buy again. A well-executed complaint handling process pays off. Resolution time, skills and knowledge of a complaint handler, and fair resolution are all key criteria for satisfaction.

Going-for-the-gold complaint resolution is not an easy process. Quick response is vital. ASQC conducted a study on the optimal complaint resolution time. It found a dramatic increase in customer defection if a complaint was not resolved within three days.[4]

British Airways has one of the best complaint systems in the business. The project is directed by Charles Weiser, who introduced a number of new customer loyalty programs in the late 1980s. At the point he joined, there was a backlog of 350,000 complaint letters. Now there is none. He automated information collection and helped to fix the problems. A customer letter is immediately scanned into a computer and a service representative calls the customer once he or she has checked the flight on the computer log to find the problem. Most responses are provided by phone, but some have to be escalated to upper management. British Airways receives 3000 cases per month in the mail, and the standard is to respond to 95 percent of these within three days.[5]

Of those who have a service problem, complainants are much more likely to fly on the airline again than those who did not complain. British Airways' top complainer has communicated with the airline 58 times. These complainants are loyal British Airways flyers. The "Come Fly With Me" program started in March 1994. Customer service reps will fly with frequent complainers and ask them what they think about the food, the cabin service, or whatever.

In the mid 1980s I had a British Airways flight that involved very poor service. I was one of the 96 percent of typical customers who walked away instead of complaining. After reading about the airline's complaint system, I decided to experiment and flew British Airways to

London a month ago. It was the best international flight I have ever experienced (out of more than 100 international flights). What a delightful surprise! Congratulations to Charles Weiser and the others who made it happen.

Exhibit 5.1 lists some of the critical issues in a good complaint handling system.

One of the best ways of handling customer complaints is the system designed by Corning Telecommunications Products Division (TPD), a winner of the 1995 Baldrige Award. Corning makes fiberglass and uses complaints to help with product and service design and refinement. Corning TPD designed its own propriety software (others use Lotus Notes) so that any salesperson, customer service individual, or employee can enter a customer complaint or compliment at any time. All employees also have access to the data.

Two elements of the complaint system design make Corning's system more actionable. One is that the screen has a template that structures the complaint information. Fields ask for specific product names, specific customer contacts, the nature of the complaint (invoice, technical, and so on) and implications (product design, service issues, training). This template helps with the retrieval of data by process owners. The second critical element is that the fields are all tied to process owners (individuals who are in charge of refining various quality issues). Process owners hold review meetings and synthesize the input at that point. They are charged with fixing the problems and held accountable in a positive way.

Anyone in Corning TPD can access the data to answer a specific question that relates to his or her function. Roll-up also happens to integrate these comments at higher-level meetings.

Lost Customer Surveys

Lost customer surveys work very well with your tier of customers that accounts for much of your revenue. For instance, beverage companies like Coca-Cola or PepsiCo might conduct lost customer research not on end users, but on those grocery or convenience stores that choose not to carry their brands. End-user studies can be done by manufacturers who keep a database on individual customers' buying behavior (Levi Strauss, Kimberly Clark, and others). Utilities might focus on companies that decide to buy their power from other operators. Engineering and construction companies conduct lost customer

Critical Issues	Hints
Collecting complaints systematically	Collect from all customer contact people—monthly is a recommended interval.
800 number and expanded hours	Companies have found that rates are cheaper after hours and it lowers their costs to have 24-hour complaint lines.
Personality characteristics in hiring	Look for patience. Use the position as a vehicle for moving up in the company.
Reporting relationships and executive involvement	The manager of customer service should be close to the top.
Training required	General Electric and Marriott both require five weeks of training. Harris Semiconductor requires even more.
Automated answers needed	Package answers for training, but customize the response.
Ownership and resolution cycle time	Corrective action needs an owner and an expected fix time. Results should be tied to performance appraisals.
Recovery incentives	Make incentives proportional to the damage. Do not bribe customers with excessive rewards.
	Taco Bell and Burger King found that people complained simply to get free coupons.
	Track receivers of discount coupons.
Rewards for complaint resolution	Provide employees rewards for quick and effective complaint resolution.
Tracking	Tracking of close times and types of complaints is important. This information then gets rolled-up into the strategic quality planning data. A Pareto chart can help separate the vital few from the trivial many complaints.

Exhibit 5.1   Critical issues in a good complaint handling system.

surveys or win/loss reports immediately after a lost bidding process. The win/loss report is passed on to relevant groups and salespeople. They may also do this if they suddenly aren't receiving requests for proposals from old customers.

MBNA, a Delaware-based credit card company, started a lost customer program in the mid-1980s. MBNA has a special unit that calls customers who have recently dropped MBNA's credit card. By working through the problems on-the-spot that caused customers to drop the card, MBNA recovers about 50 percent of the customers.[6] Partly as a result of this, MBNA keeps its customers twice as long as the industry average. Likewise, MBNA's defection rate is the lowest in the industry. MBNA's industry ranking went from 38th to fourth, and its profits increased 16-fold.[7]

The lost customer survey is one of the most powerful tools you can use to recapture customers who are in the process of defecting. It is vitally important that you see this tool as research, not a recovery technique. If your customers feel that you are really trying to sell them, instead of finding out what their problems are and fixing them, you discredit your process and irritate the very customers you want to recapture.

Defining who is a lost customer is the starting point. You need to factor out seasonal, one-time customers so you don't imply that you don't know what their buying cycle is. Start with your accounting system. Identify those customers who haven't bought from you within a specified period of time. Then have the salespeople factor out those seasonal or special customers who have defected for special reasons.

Another critical element is timing. The closer the survey is to the decision, the better. You need to figure out your customers' buying cycles. A credit card or cellular phone company can spot lost customers within days or weeks of the decision to decrease usage or drop (credit card use intervals are easily derived from transaction reports). A frequent flyer who defects is easy to spot within days or weeks. Large-lead-time contracts (telecommunications, engineering, utilities) will find lost customer surveys less able to recover clients immediately. The data are critical for prevention, but expectations need to be lowered for an immediate return on investment.

Then call those individuals, introduce yourself, and say, "We noticed you haven't purchased anything from us for x amount of time. The purpose of this research is to understand what happened." Then listen.

The caliber of the researcher who conducts lost customer surveys has to be much more sophisticated than someone who asks structured questions in telephone customer perceptual research. The interviewer needs to know the people, products, and divisions in your company. The person needs to be able to follow the customers as they tell their story and dig for back-of-the-mind information. These interviews are more like counseling sessions than mass marketing research.

The researcher also needs excellent common sense. Embedded in the customers' stories are usually issues that could be fixed immediately and may recapture them. The researcher needs to be able to say, "Would you like me to help you see if we can resolve this issue to your satisfaction? I can call Person X and see what we can do." Then the researcher needs a close relationship with key people in the organization. The individual needs to be able to call appropriate managers and enlist their help. Standards for fixing problems need to be clearly identified to managers. Just as complaint handling systems may put a three-day turnaround time on a plan of action or answer, so should lost customer systems. Then the managers or involved employees need to be recognized for their success stories in retrieving lost customers.

The researcher(s) need to tally the key reasons why customers defect. Cluster analysis works well for sorting through the copious notes that come from lost customer surveys. A Pareto chart can then be developed to show the vital few reasons for defection. This will be used in the strategic quality planning retreat to get the whole view of customer satisfiers and dissatisfiers.

One method for measuring who is a lost customer is as follows:

- Decide on your buying cycle.
- Define when a customer is likely to be lost (days, months, years).
- Check your customer list and extract lost customers.
- Take the lost customers and evaluate any special circumstance (needs to be done by sales manager or sales rep). Special circumstances include going out of business, moving, and so on.
- Calculate your attrition rate by dividing the total number of customers in that last period by the number who are lost customers.

Customer Attrition Analysis

Customer (and employee) attrition needs to be tracked in hard data. Thus, a definition of what constitutes a lost customer is a start. Attrition should be calculated on at least a quarterly basis.

Synchronize your hard data measures so they are all either monthly, quarterly, or yearly. That will make it easier to superimpose charts on each other and conduct cross analysis.

Hard data of customer attrition allows you to see if you are improving your retention rate. Hard data also allows you to compare your various locations to see which one is doing better than another.

Have the various units (divisions or locations) look at their attrition chart and comment about what was happening prior to a dramatic increase or drop in customer attrition. Many times management, policy, or quality measure changes will be apparent. Attrition analysis can be done any time. It is especially useful during or before the strategic quality retreat.

Relating customer attrition to profits, market share, and employee attrition is especially interesting. We have repeatedly found high correlations between employee and customer attrition, and between low customer attrition and high growth in market share in a high-touch service, such as retail, hotels, and so on. Increasing defects in quality measures precede increases in customer defections. Regression analysis is appropriate to discern relationships between these measures. If you don't know how to conduct regression analysis, recruit a statistician. The strategic quality planning chapter will also show you how to use a simple eyeball process to look for relationships in these trend lines.

Desired Quality Tools

Customer Satisfaction Survey

The primary benefit of this survey is that it can track trends and help you focus on major improvement and marketing efforts. Quantifiable questions are asked so that the answers can be extrapolated over a wider customer base—if sampling is done properly.

As was mentioned earlier, *Measuring Customer Satisfaction* provides an in-depth look at survey question design.[8] *Measuring and Managing Customer Satisfaction: Going for the Gold* is intended to be used in conjunction with Hayes' book. Hayes covers sampling technique, question ambiguity, and scientific issues more deeply.

Several additional elements of a good customer satisfaction survey are as follows:

• Determine what is important to your target customers.

- Match the deployment of your survey to your type of service or product.

- Adjust your questions according to the stages of buying behavior.

- Sample more of your frequent-use customers than your infrequent users.

- Use a statistical sampling process to sample a wider band of customers.

- Determine how often to survey and what incentives are necessary.

- Figure out who should conduct the interviews.

- Decide on the sample size.

- Set your confidence level.

The rest of the chapter will help you understand the importance of good questions. You will see also that in-depth tools and deployment are necessary for sophisticated services, products, and customers in a going-for-the-gold CSS. Third, you will see how silly some questions are, depending upon where you are in a buying cycle.

Determine What Is Important to Your Target Customers.   The customer satisfaction survey tracks satisfaction for your going-for-the-gold CSS. The report card approach doesn't mean it is the most powerful instrument for customer retention. It does mean it is the easiest single tool with which to measure trends and compare data. Thus, this centerpiece tool needs to be asking the right questions so that the improvement focus within the company relates to what is important to customers.

Yet it is surprising to see how few companies first did research on what customers deemed important. Quality has become a fundamental drive globally. In many companies in the United States the effort has gone as far as training employees in quality awareness. During July and August 1994, Gallup conducted telephone interviews with 403 hospital department managers, 352 elementary and secondary school principals, 316 department of motor vehicles (DMV) managers, and 301 managers in manufacturing and service businesses to gather data to compare health care, public sector, and education to mainstream business. Nearly every hospital (94 percent) had a quality program.

Sixty-six percent of schools, 28 percent of DMVs, and 58 percent of general businesses surveyed had formal programs.[9] The rhetorical question is, "How many of these started with their customers to determine what is important for them to track?"

Unless customers are asked about their priorities, many of these team efforts result in changes that do not affect the bottom line. Companies typically don't have enough resources to make all the improvements simultaneously. Why not focus on those that are valued by customers? For instance, one bank decided that it would improve customer service by doing smile training with tellers. The problem was that customers cared more about how long they waited in line. By the time the customer arrived at the teller's window, the additional friendliness was actually irritating.

Many companies have made the mistake of relying on internal managers or salespeople to answer the question for their clients, "What is important to you about this service or product?" Surveys of managers and sales on what is important to their clients produces different results than the clients' own responses. I have asked both groups (managers and clients) to list what their customers would say is most important to them in industries including dentistry, health insurance, airlines, banks, financial advisors, software programs, computers, engineering services, distribution, fast food, real estate, temporary personnel services, hotels, and others. The "what's important" overlap between the person on the inside of the industry and (potential) customers is typically only 20 percent to 40 percent. Managers and salespeople tend to confuse their own strengths with the totality of customer needs. Including competitors' customers in this sample is vital to understanding customers.

One group of airline managers, for instance, guessed that on-time departures and arrivals, flight attendant service, and food were the key satisfiers. Frequent flyers said frequent flyer points, ease of check-in, problem solving, and quick baggage handling were actually at the top of their lists. The airline was spending thousands of dollars on getting airplanes out within two minutes of departure time.

Thus, the profitable service quality companies follow this rule:

> *Focus continuous improvement efforts on what your customers say is important to them.*

AT&T Consumer Communication Systems (CCS) provides long-distance services to 80 million people. It experienced a major turn-around in market share after it learned this lesson. The increasingly higher customer satisfaction scores of AT&T CCS did not translate to increasingly higher market share. Just the opposite: Quality and customer satisfaction measures were going through the ceilings. Market share was going down precipitously. So how can satisfaction go up and market share go down? It all has to do with what questions you ask and how you look at the data.

Joe Nacchio, CEO of AT&T CSS, helped save AT&T from its precipitous slide in market share against MCI and Sprint. AT&T CCS had been amassing data for years on customer preferences and satisfaction measures. Each department looked at its scientific data separately. Nacchio told the executives to go away for a month, look at all the data at once, and come back with a report on why AT&T's long-distance satisfaction report cards were so stellar but customers were defecting in droves. The executives returned with an answer. Customers wanted simplicity, lower costs, and emotional appeal in the advertising. Thus was born a redesign of its pricing structure and an ad campaign that featured Whitney Houston in the True Voice campaigns.[10] Nacchio said that AT&T learned the lesson of focusing on what was important to the customer.

GTE Directories won the Baldrige Award in 1994. Marilyn Carlson mentioned that GTE finally asked its clients what attributes about its service were important.[11] Previously, the survey questions focused on what GTE management believed was important to customers. GTE managers had assumed that the technical quality of the printed page in the Yellow Pages was the most critical attribute. GTE Directories spent $15 million on a new web press in Los Angeles, California.

Meanwhile, the advertisers were hungry for consultative sales service rather than hard-line closing skills and wanted results from their advertising. None of the questions on the survey had focused on these two issues. GTE went back to its advertisers and finally asked the question, "What would you like us to measure in satisfaction?" The survey results allowed GTE to re-focus its money and efforts on consultative sales training and tracking results from the ads. New phone numbers were listed in the ads so that responses could be tracked. Market share went up. GTE directories are preferred in 271 out of the 274 markets where they are offered.[12]

Many surveys focus on issues that affect frontline employees instead of issues that involve tougher decisions made at higher levels. If you conduct customer satisfaction research, you have to confront yourself with a tough question.

What if you find your battery needs a new car?

How do you understand what is important to your key customers? Ask and observe. The answers may confront you with tougher issues, like changes in facilities or product or service design. This sounds simple, but it is the most complicated piece of your customer research. If you simply ask people to rate the level of importance (1 = low to 5 = high), they will say that almost everything is important, either a four or five.

The best way to find out what is important to your key customers is simply to ask the question, "What would you like us to track?" If you ask this question of enough of your customers you will find recurrent themes. A random sample of at least 30 customers is minimum for a key customer list of less than 300.

A less direct way is to use a focus interview (one customer at a time) or focus group and ask the customer(s) to describe *critical incidences* of using your product or service. Ask them: "Please describe a situation when you used a [bank, airline, cellular phone, engineering service or whatever] and had a good experience." Then use the Japanese tool called *five whys*. The five-why tool is merely another name for in-depth probing. You keep asking "why?" in creative ways.

- When someone says the tellers were good, you ask "What made them good?"
- When the customer replies, "The teller knew the answers," you ask them to explain the nature of the questions or how long it took to figure out the right answer.

At the end of this probing you have a clear idea of *exactly* what satisfied the customer. You ask the same customer for a second positive critical incident. Then you ask for a couple of negative examples and probe for irritants. Critical incidences make it much easier for customers to access their deeper memories for details and the emotional issues involved in the transaction.

Hands-on training in how to probe in critical incidences can help those who will be conducting focused interviews. The technique can be easily taught in an hour. Monitoring the first focused interviews helps to refine the technique. Analyzing this qualitative information gathered from the focused interview is covered under cluster and decibel analysis in chapter 7.

> *Use qualitative measures with a few customers to develop questions.*
>
> *Use quantitative measures across your customer base to get answers.*

Qualitative measures are open-ended questions on surveys, focus interviews or groups, employee contacts with customers, and so on. Some of the best CSS information comes from qualitative measures because *qualitative measures are driven by customers.* Questions come from customers, not from predesigned quantitative surveys that box customers into a rating scale. Qualitative measures are quantified through cluster analysis, check sheets, and decibel analysis. Verbatim analysis provides a computerized word check to find certain words or phrases. GTE uses verbatim analysis for large database searches.

Armstrong Building Products Operation, winner of the 1995 Baldrige Award, uses a computer software program called FACT. Any employee can make comments about any customer at any time. Armstrong found that innovation was vitally important to its customers when it looked at the themes on these comments. It also saw that new product introductions were highly related to profits. Thus, it accelerated its new product development process.[13]

Collect all the results from qualitative measures you have taken so far. If you haven't done any, do focused interviews with at least 30 of your gold customers who are selected randomly from that tier. Ask them what they want you to track. Let them talk while you take notes, then probe. Use a list of your service or product features to probe about the importance of those features. Using 100 points to distribute across the choices helps you weight the scores later. Then focus your customer satisfaction survey on the critical factors for success. You can then translate those critical factors for success into your internal quality measures, department by department.

Double-check your survey questions to see if you are measuring the obvious. One fast food client researched customers and found that they liked their french fries warm. "Warm" translated into 94°. The temperature of the fries was programmed into the heat of the oil and length of the cooking process. The Japanese call this *poke yoke*—idiot proof. You might test later to see if customer preferences change. Waiting lines at drive thrus are also easy to measure. Have the customer define the specification. Internal measures can then track it. You don't need to waste precious questions on a systematic survey for those issues that can be measured in other ways. Many of these issues are in Kano's expected quality zone.

Double-check to see that expected quality issues are not the major portion of your questions. You usually compete at the desired and excited quality levels. If customers define fast food as "being served within three minutes of arrival," set that as your standard. Use your surveys to probe other issues that may affect choosing your fast food over another's. Those issues could include lighting, the music played in the background, the size of the tables, parking, menu choices, or other, tougher issues. The law of diminishing returns sets in when you try to compete with other fast food restaurants on whether customers are served in 90 seconds or 80 seconds. Meanwhile, they may select other fast food restaurants on other issues—lighting, music, or whatever.

The same applies to high-tech industries. Some electronics, integrated circuit, or power supply companies tout all the resources being provided to achieve six-sigma defect levels or a 15-year life span for their product. Yet their technology is obsolete in two to three years. Meanwhile, little attention is given to the invoice system, which has been a very hot customer dissatisfier.

> *Watch for the law of diminishing returns*
> *in setting your quality goals.*

Match the Deployment of Your Survey to Your Type of Service or Product. Phoning customers for a customer satisfaction survey yields vastly different results than a written survey for complex services or products (if you probe). You cannot get in-depth information from people on a written survey. Most people don't like to write.

Several of our hospital clients use a six- to eight-page survey and get in-depth information. The interviewer is a welcome relief to boredom for people who are in the hospital. They had tried mailing that same survey to active executives after they left the hospital and received less than a 10 percent response. Filling captive time or relieving boredom yields more patience with your questions.

> *Written surveys are excellent for report cards, complex questions, or a simple feedback process. Phone or in-person surveys are your best vehicles for in-depth information.*

Adjust Your Questions According to the Stages of Buying Behavior. Questions need to be appropriate to where the customer is in the buying cycle—a first-time buyer, new user, or loyal customer. Point-of-purchase questions measure the selection criteria and buying experience. A person at the checkout counter in a grocery store may ask a few questions about why customers bought one product over another. Usage questions help you determine why customers aren't using more of your product or service. Field research helps you determine how people actually use your product or service and how you can improve its user-friendly aspects.

In usage research, many companies find surprises. Roto Rooter is usually pictured as a plumbing company. Yet a respectable part of its business is retrieving wedding rings. One client was in the carbon dioxide business. The foundation of its company was supplying restaurants and bars the fizz for their drinks. When it looked at its market segments, it found that the highest revenues and profits had now switched to providing carbon dioxide for balloons rather than servicing the restaurants and bars.

Calibrate your questions according to these stages of buying behavior. Exhibit 5.2 illustrates the stages of customer buying and the appropriate focus of the questions. Point-of-purchase questions need to focus on why the person bought. New users' questions need to focus on ease of installation, manuals, use, and how the product or service compares to competitors that the buyer may have recently worked with. Loyal customer research allows the researcher to find out the latent features, the nuances of the product or feature attributes, the subtle irritants and pleasures, and ideas for new product or service design.

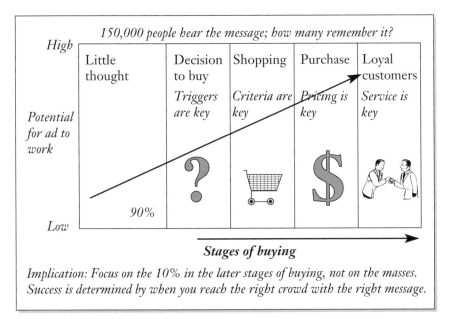

Exhibit 5.2 Stages of customer buying.

Several food manufacturers are using point-of-purchase coupons and cameras to see how customers buy.[14] A point-of-purchase coupon or product demo is either a video description of the product or actual sample and coupon that is handed out in the grocery store. Point-of-purchase advertising programs are now a $17 billion industry.

Observing someone at the point of purchase is an appropriate tool for low relationship products because it is relatively nonintrusive on the consumer's time and yet gives objective data about buying influences. Eastman Kodak found in its observation research that consumers looked at the box of film for an unusually long period of time while evaluating their purchase decision. The importance of having the competitive edge over the competition, or listing benefits on the package, became apparent.[15]

Consider what you can do to capture that point-of-purchase information. Nearly 70 percent of grocery store purchases are impulse buys.[16] McDonald's found that most people make a decision to visit McDonald's within three minutes of arriving at the door. Both do intercept research after people have purchased. How can you assess why your customers make the decision to buy your product or service rather than your competitor's—especially at the exact point of purchase?

The best vehicle for this knowledge is to train your cash register or reservation people to ask the question, "What features helped you choose our product or service?" Then gather the data. Further elaboration is provided in the win/loss analysis tool described in the tool tip section

Don't expect people to understand much about your product or service if they haven't used it extensively. You may wait a couple of weeks or months after the point of purchase to ask questions about the competition in a telephone survey. Microsoft calls a random sample of newly registered software users and asks about installation and competitors' features about a month after purchase.

Ask questions appropriate for your customers' understanding of your service or product. A college would not want to ask freshmen about the relevance of the curriculum or how the curriculum prepared them for an occupation. These questions would be appropriate for alumni who have been in their jobs for several years. Appropriate questions for freshmen would be about how they made their selection, the ease of first-time registration, the quality of the orientation, and the quality of their initial courses. Questions on how to smooth the transition would also be appropriate.

One professional organization held a series of focus groups to conduct an in-depth analysis of what they could do better to retain customers. The tool was well-matched to the purpose. The problem was that they asked questions like, "What led you to select this professional organization over your other choices?" It's an excellent question for participants who had just signed on, but a poor question for all of us who made the purchase decision more than 10 years ago. The nature of the rest of the questions was similar—point-of-purchase questions. Members of the group couldn't remember why they made their choice. The objective of the focus group was to find ways to improve service levels to better retain existing customers. The selection of a focus group as the tool was right. The selection of sophisticated users as participants was right. The questions were wrong.

After point of purchase, usage becomes a critical factor for profitability. How many credit cards do you have that just sit in your wallet or desk? What would increase your weekend visits to a certain hotel chain? What would encourage you to use your cellular phone more or make more long distance phone calls? These usage questions are best measured a few months after purchase or after a major change in usage. Companies like AT&T Universal Card Services and Cellular

One spend considerable effort to research what would increase usage. Special research projects with focused interviews are effective at this point. Written surveys tend to receive low response rates and provide inadequate depth or less-than-honest information.

The honesty issue in usage surveys is subtle. Some cost-conscious managers might have trouble admitting that they don't use one airline as much as they could because the airline has a three-year limit on frequent flyer miles. The managers may respect the service level the airline has achieved and feel a bit guilty about their real reason. If someone created a safe interview environment for those managers to be honest, they might be honest. A written survey may be too self-incriminating. Any single one of those business frequent-flyer customers may have a lifetime worth of more than $1 million. At high levels, that single passenger may influence the organization and be worth hundreds of millions of dollars. Is making the survey personal important to airlines?

Field research is done to understand how customers use your product or service. This field research provides valuable input into design. In a speech given by Yoshinori, a quality guru in Japan, to the Executive Mission I was on in 1992, he talked about the extensive use of field observation in Japan for product and service innovations. Japanese companies call this observation *use engineering*. The way people use products makes a significant difference in how they engineer products. They found it difficult to predict how people use power shovels, for instance. Some use them to destroy buildings, and that takes certain swing strengths. Others use them to dig dirt, and that takes different strengths. Some of the washing machine manufacturers found that families used the washing machine to clean potatoes. Design requirements changed. Bridgestone gained much of its dominance in the tire industry by putting stations at the bottom of the rugged Oregon mountains and doing scientific field tests when truck drivers came in with damaged tires. Instead of the theoretical lab tests done by U.S. tire companies, the Japanese engineers could observe what the exact conditions were for the damaged tires. They changed the composition to withstand those wear-and-tear conditions.

In Spa Resort Hawaiian, the first hotel to win the Deming Prize, managers put cameras behind the check-in counter and timed how long it took for people to get restless as they were checking in. They then gauged their staffing to accommodate the optimal waiting period. Field observation is critical for high-performing companies. Tires are a high-relationship product for a logger. Waiting line frustration means a lot to busy executives. Lost time can mean lost revenues.

Sample More of Your Frequent-Use Customers Than Your Infrequent Users. The purpose of segmenting your customer base in the previous chapter was to focus on your gold clients. You want to sample your gold clients much more heavily than those who aren't. Why?

> *The act of surveying helps build partnerships with customers.*

Just calling or sending a written survey to customers communicates that you care about their feedback. If the process is done well, those customers become invested in your success. That means that they take time out apart from the survey to give feedback, talk about your company to friends, and do what they can to help you. While this is not the purpose of collecting data, it is a by-product. Increasing your sample size for a high-relationship product or service is in your best interests. You are both inadvertently marketing and gathering data simultaneously.

> *If at all possible, get input from all of your solid gold customers.*

If you don't have a database of your customers and can't tell who uses you most, find out. Sixty-six percent of senior marketing executives said they already are using a marketing database to improve relationships with customers and prospects. And of the 34 percent who don't, 48 percent plan to build one.[17] Qualifying information on a customer satisfaction survey can help you find vital information. You need to find out whether customers are frequent users by asking a question resembling the following:

> *How frequently to you use our product or service?*
>
> ❏ *Several times a week*   ❏ *Several times a year*
>
> ❏ *Several times a month*   ❏ *Never*

The categories in the answer will differ, depending upon your typical buying interval. Offer a drawing or incentive for filling out your questionnaire and providing a name and address. Then keep information about those frequent customers in a database so you can do direct mail marketing. Contests or special discounts to frequent users (such as used by Walden Book Stores and Brentanos) will also foster database tracking.

The question of what percentage of each segment you should sample is important. I encourage companies to sample at least 100 percent of their gold clients and be rigorous enough to obtain an 80 percent response rate. It takes considerable effort to get a return rate of 80 percent. If you use a written survey, it takes calling customers to let them know you are sending the survey and then reminding the individual customers their survey is overdue until they send it in. Most companies average at least three calls to obtain 80 percent. Telephone surveys are actually easier to complete at that response rate. If you are aiming for an 80 percent response rate, the costs are about the same between written and telephone.

If you segment your customers, you will find the numbers of target customers are not that great. Coca-Cola has millions of end users. Yet the key to its success is the distribution channel—grocery stores, restaurants, and convenience stores. Your distribution channel will involve hundreds or thousands rather than millions of people. Divided among several regions, each region then inherits just hundreds of target customers to track. If each retail chain is worth millions of dollars to Coca-Cola, is a telephone call at regular intervals worth the expense? Over a lifetime, each of those customers can easily be worth billions rather than millions of dollars.

Consumer product companies like Coca-Cola, Procter & Gamble, Colgate Palmolive, General Mills, Kellogg's, and many other packaged goods companies have done an excellent job of consumer research. Consumer research, however, is different from partnership research. Consumer research may look for preferences then get translated to quality measures. Is the consistency of the syrup the same? Does the quality of the water make a difference in the beer or beverage? (Yes!) The main reason to survey end users is about product/service preferences, packaging, advertising issues, customers' top-of-mind awareness, pricing, and availability. These research projects are different from the partnership and personal measurement of distributors. You can see how the CSS design has to reflect the nature of the business and be multi-tiered, if necessary.

Use a Statistical Sampling Process to Sample a Wider Band of Customers. Sampling your entire customer base is done if you have too many customers to survey all of them efficiently. Sampling may vary according to the objectives for your CSS plan and how many customers you have in each segment. Some sampling choices include full database sampling (consensus sampling), random sampling, stratified random sampling, quota sampling, and convenience sampling.

• *Full database sampling.* For instance, if the purpose of your CSS is to build partnerships with your 300 gold distribution clients, you need to consider sampling all of the clients on your gold client list. Many companies find that their key clients talk to each other. In the early years we discovered that sampling even 70 percent of a gold customer database elicited complaints from those who didn't get surveyed.

USAA in San Antonio markets insurance, banking services, and mutual funds. It sends out 500,000 questionnaires to a sample of its 2.5 million customers. More than 60 percent respond, and USAA follows up.[18] Customers asked for a growth and income mutual fund, so USAA launched one. It was an instant success.

• *Random sampling.* Random sampling means that the entire customer base has a known and equal chance of being included in the sample. Large companies like AT&T CCS use random sampling because their end users number more than 80 million. Random sampling can be done by assigning customers numbers and then generating a computer list of random numbers. Drawing those numbers from a hat can be a small-company approach.

The Harris Poll surveys about 1500 people in the United States and extrapolates across the rest of the nation with a level of confidence of plus or minus 5 percent. Nielson Ratings for television typically take diaries from about 1000 television viewers in a population of one million. Sampling procedures in these polls are rigorous and the total populations are large, so they can get by with smaller numbers.

• *Stratified random sampling.* Stratified random sampling starts with segmenting your customers. You can segment by product line, customer type, usage, geography, profitability, growth, revenues, or whatever dimension makes sense. Within each segment you choose a random sample, so that each person in the sample has a known and equal chance of being drawn.

- *Quota sampling.*   Managers may want quotas within a sampling strata or across the entire customer base. The quotas may include male/female splits, certain frequency of users, and functional splits (engineers, distributors, and so on). Quota sampling can distort results, whereas stratified random sampling usually curtails the probability of bias.

- *Convenience sampling.*   Random sampling allows you to draw conclusions from a sample of your entire population. Some companies use convenient samples. These convenience questionnaires are everywhere—at stores, car rental agencies, hotels, banks, and retail outlets. These forms tend to function more as reactive complaint systems than proactive customer research. It takes a motivated (angry or pleased) individual to participate. The information can be useful in devising questions to use in a more scientific sampling process. Company strategy can easily be thrown off by just using convenience sampling. Use it in conjunction with the other multipoint measures.

Determine How Often to Survey and What Incentives Are Necessary. The frequency of survey measurement depends on several factors.

- How much your customers are willing to participate
- How important your service or product is to your customers' success
- How quickly your technology changes
- How far ahead (or behind) the competition you are

Wainwright benchmarked Solectron when it was designing its system. Solectron surveyed weekly. Jo Sanders, head of customer service for Wainwright, mentioned that its customer base wouldn't tolerate weekly surveying. Wainwright decided to survey once a month and had to sell this to some reluctant customers.

Other factors include how important your product or service is to your customers. The less important the product or service, the more you may have to use incentives. I found that cash drawings with physicians work well in getting their cooperation on feedback. The price needs to be sizable enough ($1000 or more) and the odds reasonable enough to be a motivation.

Decide Who Should Conduct the Interviews. If the customer survey is a telephone survey, the company has a choice of whether to hire a neutral outside company to do the survey, use its own people, or distribute the interviewing among employees. Our experience at Competitive Edge is that companies tend to evolve through these three stages: (1) a neutral outside organization is useful if the customers are hesitant to express the full extent of their negative input in the beginning; (2) as customer service and the products improve, that negative input is less of an issue; and (3) the interviewing can be done by an inside (but neutral) reseach function.

The benefit of training your employees to conduct a customer satisfaction phone interview is that they hear directly from customers. Likewise, probing improves if insiders are used. If you are surveying business-to-business customers, you will need highly skilled interviewers. Consumer research can get by with less-skilled interviewers. If selected well, those employees know where to go to pull the strings that make change happen. The employees still need to be neutral researchers for this to be effective. A separate research entity that reports to the COO helps.

Business-to-business research requires the skills of higher-level people who can get around the formidable walls put up by secretaries, ad-lib probing questions, and understand business issues. U.S. consumer companies have traditionally used market research companies to measure consumer reactions. Part-time college students (where I started in this business) are typically used to keep costs down. Not a good idea for interviewing higher-level executive decision makers! Shop wisely for an outside research group if you have business-to-business customers.

Business-to-business researchers beware:

Match interviewer skills to levels in the customer organization you will be researching.

Many consumer research companies claim that they do this. Test the interviewers yourself.

Be part of the interviewers' selection and training.

Role-play. This is extremely important.

The other option is to train insiders to do the interviewing. This works well for customer satisfaction measurement but not for perceptual research, because noncustomers are included in the perceptual research sample and the phone survey needs to be anonymous. One example of using insiders for customer satisfaction in a distributed survey process is the system at Lexus. Each of the 250 employees at Lexus' U.S. headquarters in Torrance, California, must make at least five phone calls per month to customers who recently took delivery of a Lexus. The employees always ask them if they're satisfied—and if not, why not.[19] The advantage to insider query (if surveyors are well-trained) is that they get to hear the emotional content directly.

At AT&T Universal Card Services, which won the Baldrige Award in 1991, executives are required to listen to these telephone surveys at regular intervals. Zytec has its executives call a certain number of its top 1700 customers every month.[20] Hearing customers first-hand helps management take action.

Decide on the Sample Size.   Many statistical books include tables that determine the sample size needed for making probability determinations. Earl Naumann in *Customer Satisfaction Measurement and Management* talked about how determining the sample size is not as simple as the statistics books imply.[21] Budgets, internal availability of resources, schedule, and pressure to come out with timely product/service introductions all factor in. Many companies will set a budget and say "Sample as many as you can for $60,000." A third of that cost would be taken in overhead expenses. Thus, the remaining $40,000 would need to be applied in a way that optimizes the usefulness of the data. If there are severe budget constraints, I encourage companies to just pick off their vital few customers and do a better job focusing on high-return-on-investment customers. It is much more important to get a representative sampling of your key client base or strata than to sample your entire client list.

Set Your Confidence Level.   The confidence level indicates a level of certainty about the results. At a 95-percent confidence level, the researcher is 95 percent certain that the data are accurate. Increased confidence levels require increased sample sizes. If the stakes are high (large capital expenditures in a new product or distribution channel, high physical risks in a new medical product, and so on), the confi-

Population size	Sample size (Number of respondents needed)
100	80
200	132
500	218
1000	278
1,500	306
2,000	323
5,000	347
10,000	370
20,000	377

Exhibit 5.3   Sample size requirements at 95-percent confidence level.

dence levels need to be very high. You see confidence levels in many of the Harris Polls at the end of the results table.

Confidence level is dependent upon the size of the sample. Exhibit 5.3 shows the relationship between population size and required number of respondents to achieve a 95-percent confidence level.

Even more important is the persistence with which you go after your sample. Accepting a 10-percent return rate on a 30-percent sample is not worth your trouble. The 10 percent who happen to respond could represent a biased sample (complainers) and not be fully representative. Use your resources to obtain at least an 80-percent return on whatever sample size you choose. Achieving an 80-percent return rate is done by letting customers know you will be sampling them, offering some incentive for participating, and persisting when they are either not easily reached or don't return the questionnaire.

Transaction Surveys

Transaction surveys are surveys that are conducted on-the-spot as a transaction occurs. The simple survey is done upon delivery of the goods, after the selling transaction, immediately after a repair, and so on. Transaction surveys are discussed more fully in the tool tip section. They are more real time than customer satisfaction surveys, since employees can fix problems as they arise. Training employees to do transaction surveys, recording the data, and using them for change is one of the most powerful tools in the tool kit. Unfortunately, it is one of the least-used tools.

Excited Quality Tools

Excited quality tools are those that put more emphasis on managing customer satisfaction than measuring it. Still, they can be used to measure satisfaction informally in fun settings. Those creative ways of staying in touch include customer events, joined-at-the hip programs, and customer training. The only limit to these creative tools is the size of your imagination. These tools focus on the art of pleasing customers, not the science.

High-relationship businesses that are successful have found some very creative ways of staying in touch with their solid gold customers. Even though these aren't scientific, they provide a rich source of information. Many frequent users know more about a company's nuances than any single individual in the company.

So how does Marriott take advantage of this resource? Most of the key hotels have either a monthly or weekly cocktail party for their Platinum guests who happen to be staying with them that night. The managers, sales staff, chefs, and some supervisors attend. We freely both praise them and offer suggestions—some of which we have learned from positive experiences at other hotels. While a cocktail party may not seem terribly original, the systematic use of it to ask marketing and satisfaction questions is.

Compaq Computer, number one in personal computer sales in 1994, is the wildly successful darling of Wall Street. Gian Carlo Bisone, vice president for North American marketing, says, "There's no substitute for face-to-face communication." In September 1993, Compaq spent $250,000 on a fancy, four-day trade show where 400 of its best customers were invited. It drew an additional 6000 people. It gave Compaq a wonderful opportunity to mix solid gold customers with potential customers.[22] What made this trade show special was the focus on displaying new products, educating customers, and entertaining them. Compaq went to great expense to include customers in its product launch.

In June 1994, Saturn held a gala (though rainy) reunion with 44,000 of its proud Saturn owners. The customer intimacy (and feedback) is a vital way to both learn and gain ground against the competition. These creative ways to integrate customer research, customer satisfaction public relations, and fun are powerful. *Interaction* and *intimacy with customers* are the watch words of the twenty-first century. Saturn also uses hands-on local events like Saturn car clubs, car clinics, and others to create word-of-mouth advertising and customer loyalty.

Summary

The key tools for your quest for gold were discussed in detail in this chapter. Expected tools, such as complaint systems, lost customer surveys, and customer attrition analysis, help you prevent your gold from washing downstream. The customer satisfaction survey was highlighted under the desired quality tools. After you determine what your customers deem important to track over time, you need to choose whether it will be via a written or phone survey or both. Questions need to reflect the customers' familiarity with your service or product, or the stage of their buying behavior. Suggestions were given for sampling your customers according to how important that segment is to your growth. Decisions on the frequency of the survey depend on how quickly your industry moves and what the buying cycles are for your customers. Who does the interview, whether it is a telephone survey or written survey, also needs to be adapted to the sophistication and technical level of the customer.

The next chapter covers how to use the tools efficiently and effectively.

Notes

1. Technical Assistance Research Programs, *Consumer Complaint Handling in America: An Update Study* (Washington, D.C.: Office of Consumer Affairs, 31 March 1986).

2. Pamela Gordon, "Customer Satisfaction Research Reaps Rewards," *Quality* 32 (May 1993): 39–41. (Pamela Gordon is president of Technology Forecasters in Berkeley, California.)

3. Technical Assistance Research Programs, *Consumer Complaint Handling in America*.

4. Brian J. LeHouillier, "ASQC Baseline Customer Satisfaction Survey" (presentation to ASQC staff, October 1993).

5. James Brown, "British Airways 'Caress' Passengers with Customer Complaint Program," *Airline Marketing News*, 2 March 1994, 8.

6. Larry Armstrong and William Symonds, "Beyond May I Help You," *Business Week*, 25 October 1991, 100–102.

7. Frederick F. Reichheld and W. Earl Sasser Jr., "Zero Defections: Quality Comes to Service," *Harvard Business Review* (September-October 1990): 107.

8. Bob E. Hayes, *Measuring Customer Satisfaction: Development and Use of Questionnaires* (Milwaukee: ASQC Quality Press, 1992.)

9. John Ryan, "Alternative Routes on the Quality Journey: ASQC/Gallup Survey Compares Diffustion of Quality Attitudes and Practices in Diverse Organizations," *Quality Progress* 27, no. 12 (December 1994): 37.

10. Joe Nacchio, CEO of AT&T Customer Communication Systems, interview by author, Washington, D.C., 7 February 1995.

11. Marilyn Carlson, GTE Directories, interview by author, Washington, D.C., 6 February 1995.

12. James Overstreet, "Winners Court Customers, Listen to Workers: GTE Award Carves Road to Improvement," *USA Today*, 19 October 1994, 4B.

13. Mike Conner, operations accountant at Armstrong Building Products Operation, interview by author, Washington, D.C., 6 February 1996.

14. Leah Haran, "Point-of-Purchase: Marketers Getting with the Program," *Advertising Age*, 25 October 1993, 33.

15. Michael Lottie, director of consumer research at Eastman Kodak, interview by author, Washington, D.C., 20 February 1996.

16. Michael Corbett, *How to Make the 33 Ruthless Rules of Local Advertising Work for You* (Houston, Tex.: Breakthru Publishing, 1994).

17. "What Marketers Told Us," *The Marketing Report*, 27 February 1995, 2.

18. Terence Pare, "How to Find Out What They Want," *FORTUNE*, autumn/winter 1993, 39.

19. "Value: A New Kind of Bottom Line," *Los Angeles Times*, 14 August 1993, A37.

20. Doug Tersteeg, manager of quality at Zytec, interview by author, Redwood Falls, Minn., 22 October 1992.

21. Earl Naumann and Kathleen Giel, *Customer Satisfaction Measurement and Management* (Cincinnati, Ohio: International Thomson Publishing, 1995), 103.

22. Patricia Sellers, "The Best Way to Reach Your Buyers," *FORTUNE*, autumn/winter 1993, 14.

Chapter 6

Using the Tools: Efficient and Effective Digging

The way you use CSS tools will either enhance your relationship with your gold customers or be one more nail in your coffin. Likewise, your measurement system will do the same with your employees. They will either be motivated toward further excellence, or driven to manipulate the numbers.

Poorly designed and deployed customer satisfaction tools will raise client (and employee) expectations and create disappointment. As loyal customers, we have a tendency to expect to see our suggestions implemented when we go to the trouble of expressing them.

Thus, in Midas-touch deployment, you must do the following:

> *Manage expectations even as you measure them.*

What you don't want to imply is that you will be responsive to every complaint or that you will change your entire organization based on one individual's remarks. This is particularly difficult to manage in a complaint system in which people are angry. Training customer service people to listen and empathize without agreeing or implying immediate change is tricky.

The Midas Touch in deployment involves the following elements.

- A system designed at the top with input from the bottom
- A formal and informal system
- A system that has clear responsibilities and motivates employees

- A system that focuses on the positive
- A system that makes the data visible
- A system that properly channels the data

A System Designed at the Top

The executive committee or CSS steering committee should be the owners of the CSS. The entire organization needs one group to monitor the consistency of the tools, train the facilitators of the focus groups, hire outside consultants that provide consistency across the organization, and plan celebrations that have enough clout to serve as motivators for excellence.

A Formal and Informal System

Formalize your CSS. That doesn't mean loading it with staff members. It *does* mean publicizing the plan, process, and results. Many Japanese companies have annual quality reports and presidential reviews of results. Hundreds of U.S. companies like Xerox, AT&T, Fox Valley College, and many others have annual quality forums or team expos where quality results are paraded. Henry Bradshaw, CEO of Armstrong Building Products Operation, commented that his favorite activity of the year is going to the team expo in Amelia Island, Florida.[1] There the teams that have won local contests for their efforts and results strut their stuff by presenting how they achieved their particular improvements.

A System That Has Clear Responsibilities and Motivates Employees

In order to get the necessary motivation out of employees, executives and management must attend to two elements of deployment:

1. Involve those who will implement changes in the design.
2. Focus on the positive rather than the negative.

See Exhibit 6.1 for a list of deployment responsibilities.

Who	What
CSS steering committee	• Sets objectives of CSS measurement system • Establishes level of commitment • Communicates commitment and process to units • Retains consultant for advice (if necessary) • Asks units for hypothetical questions • Sets up initial focus groups or customer contacts • Analyzes and synthesizes the data • Designs the key questions for CSS survey • Recruits outside company for benchmark survey (if desired) • Coordinates how pricing questions will be asked or tested • Tracks complaint system and transaction results • Synthesizes data from all input systems • Designs a CSS data review process • Organizes cross-functional teams to address specific improvement projects • Considers new services/products • Designs overall celebration system • Coordinates or participates in the strategic quality planning meeting
Units or divisions	• Add questions to company CSS survey • Design own transaction surveys • Design own observation and complaint tracking systems with standards set by the CSS steering committee. • Design goals and quality measures that support strategic quality goals • Have owners of improvement initiatives • Measure cycle time of responding to complaints • Are accountable for changes needed in group
Executive committee	• Makes input about parameters of CSS plan • Determines level of company commitment (resources, people, and so on) • Selects one or two of its members to serve on CSS committee • Can be same group as CSS steering committee, but not necessarily • Makes financial, marketing, quality, and employee data available to CSS steering committee

Exhibit 6.1   Deployment responsibilities.

Tool/function	Typical owners
Integration of CSS system	CSS steering committee
Quality function deployment	Engineering or sales
Complaint	Customer service
Pricing analysis	Marketing or sales
Win/loss analysis	Sales
Customer satisfaction surveys	CSS steering committee
Transaction surveys	Departments
Expected quality measures (specifications provided by customers)	Quality control, engineering, and production

Exhibit 6.2   Tool owners.

Most readers of this book probably recognize the typical departments that act as owners of the various tools. Exhibit 6.2 shows the tools and the departments that typically own the tools.

Ownership does not mean being territorial. Ownership means that each owner coordinates input from other departments and tracks results. Measuring and managing customer satisfaction is an integrated, cross-functional effort. Otherwise, customers receive a multitude of uncoordinated queries about needs, features, and satisfaction.

Each tool usually produces queries and problems that require immediate attention for customers. Owners within functional areas are immediately appointed to take care of the issue. If ordering is a problem, the business or order entry group would have a person assigned as owner. If durability is the issue, the engineering department might be in charge with assistance from materials. These process owners would orchestrate a quality improvement team, if necessary, or resolve the issue alone. The owner is accountable as measured on his or her performance appraisal. Rewards and recognition are also imperative to drive the spirit of customer problem solving.

A System That Focuses on the Positive

Focusing on the positive means knowing how to celebrate publicly and coach privately. This is one of the largest discriminators between rigorous companies and gold CSS companies that displayed their

CSS through frontline behavior instead of just report cards (mentioned in the preface). Celebration is worth the whole chapter (chapter 9) devoted to it. This is particularly true for customer satisfaction data.

In the beginning of incorporating negative and positive feedback from customers, I found that much conditioning is needed. The following bad habits are difficult to break.

- Overfocus on the negative
- Underfocus on the positive
- Overlooking poor CSS scores if the unit is highly profitable or has high revenues
- Overlooking good CSS scores if the unit is less profitable or has lower revenues

Financial blinders are particularly hazardous. Superficial analysis has a logic of its own: If this unit or division can make so much money without making customers happy, why bother spending the extra time, money, and energy? The conclusion: We'll just ignore customer data for good performers. Stop and remember the PVA, CVA, and EVA model. If you don't attend to the early warning signs, you will be caught off-guard when financial areas crash.

Many times financial high flyers are riding on the wave of a local boom. Look at the competitors and see if they are riding that same wave. Sometimes the high profit is driven by a scrooge manager who is not letting employees invest in customers. Profit looks good, but customers are on the verge of defecting. High profits can also be driven by being a sole source. Not attending to customer satisfaction portends ill when the local economy dips, when customers get frustrated with nonresponsiveness, and when new competitors move in.

> *Don't let riding the high economic tide blind you from the rocks.*
>
> *The rocks will do serious damage when the tide goes down.*

Managers usually need some coaching on how to be supportive in down times. Allow the team or individuals with less-than-desirable numbers come up with their own root cause analysis and plan (have them assess what has worked in the other areas) and then give them time to let it work. GTE in Irvine has a policy of throwing a party when the numbers are down. The thinking is that down times are heartfelt by employees. Brief financial downturns may mean employees need special support and belief in them expressed. Thus,

> *Kiss 'em when they are down, kick 'em when they are up.*

Micromanaging negative results will demoralize even successful areas of the organization. Even the Japanese Deming Prize–winning companies I visited in 1992 (Komatsu Dresser, Juki, Nissan, Y Hewlett-Packard, and Fuji Xerox) said they had trouble with this in the beginning. Y Hewlett-Packard and Fuji Xerox are the Japanese units that handle Hewlett-Packard's and Xerox's business in the Pacific Rim.

CSS and quality data were incorporated into a presidential diagnosis and annual quality report in these Japanese companies. The president of the company spent at least 30 percent to 50 percent of his time reviewing these results with each unit and removing obstacles. Positive results are celebrated, and negative results receive coaching.

In the beginning, the executive handling of negative results was fairly brutal. Considerable energies were applied to making the coaching more supportive. Highly competitive companies (those that go for the gold) can expect to have trouble; it goes with the territory. Harsh and public hammering on negative results may create temporary gains. The dangers of brutal feedback involve future fudging of numbers, lost employees, or disregard for both the data and the people pounding on them. None of this is good for honesty, morale, and employee turnover.

A System That Makes the Data Visible

Visibility in yearly reviews is not enough. High-performing companies have more frequent reviews, based on the importance of issues to customers. More frequent reviews are also appropriate for those issues that need rapid improvement in a short period of time. Real-time reviews on key customer complaints happen daily within some of our microchip, high-tech, engineering spare parts, and hotels clients. Fast fixes are determined.

In addition, CSS data can be posted on bulletin boards on trend charts. The CSS steering committee needs to look for every opportunity to make the data more visible, through newsletters, staff meetings, "atta-boy" notes, or whatever. Robert Baer, CEO of United Van Lines, talked about one of his agents, Pete Sorenson, who gives bonuses to everyone involved in a move for which a government customer gives 100 percent of the possible points on the three criteria that government measures: on-time pickup, delivery, and no damage.[2]

> *The more visible the data, the more effective they will be.*

Your assessment system gives you the data to know where to dig. Knowing where to dig does not ensure that your employees will have the necessary energy to cut through hard rock. The system has to help motivate them to do so, or your treasure map is worthless. Too many surveys end up as piles of computer printouts on a shelf.

Keep in mind that trend charts speak for themselves if they are visible. No one likes to look at negative results posted on a bulletin board.

> *Trust the competencies of your winning crew to self-correct.*

A System That Properly Channels the Data

Whether you are using a focus group, a survey, a win/loss analysis, or any other tool, you will find three levels of data in each tool. Each level needs to be channeled appropriately to the proper recipients. Those three levels of data are the following:

1. Individual employee problems or compliments
2. Unit (market, division, department) problems or compliments
3. System or companywide problems or compliments (usually related to customer-hostile policies, culture, enforcement of quality standards, design, information systems, invoice and ordering, promotions, prices, or hiring)

Individual employee problems or compliments usually surface on surveys in the open-ended questions you ask.

- What do you like about us?

- What improvements do you suggest?

Even in focused interviews or groups, customers volunteer comments about specific employees without being asked.

Going for the gold implies that customer satisfaction is the ultimate goal of any measurement system. If the customer is having problems with an individual, the researcher has an opportunity to do something about the problem. Comments about an individual employee may have to do with an irritating behavior, a difference of opinion, or something else.

The philosophy undergirding individual complaints goes back to W. Edwards Deming. He (and J. M. Juran) maintained that 85 percent of the problems really stemmed from systems problems and 15 percent from individuals. The first avenue of root cause analysis should look for system issues—training, direction, matching employees to customers, compensation, and so on.

> *However, 15 percent of the complaints may have something to do with the individual.*

As was previously mentioned in the TARP research, 75 percent of customers defect because of the indifference of one employee, so these comments should be taken seriously (if they are expressed seriously). The researcher might give the feedback to the supervisor in a way that allows the supervisor to mediate between the customer and employee. If the issue cannot be resolved, consideration should be given to moving that customer to another employee who better fits his or her personality style. Customers have quirks that can conflict with employee quirks, even though both may be blameless. The supervisor needs to be sensitive to matching employee personalities to customer personalities. If a single individual receives a disproportionate amount of passionate complaints, corrective action should be taken with that individual. Marriott is very intolerant of employees who abuse customers: three warranted serious complaints and you are out. The seriousness of customer satisfaction is communicated by this intolerance.

Part of the CSS plan includes where the data gatherers will channel the information or unresolved issues from customers. Process owners are the first logical place. Review cycles and who will be reviewing these process owners also need to be determined. Periodic participation of CSS steering committee members in lower-level reviews helps the big picture cascade down to lower levels. The higher the status of the individual reviewing, the more impact it has. That is why high-performing Japanese company CEOs spend so much time in this process.

The CSS steering committee needs to set a review cycle so that it can monitor the collective results of key processes. That is usually done in the strategic quality planning meeting. In fast-moving or high-tech companies, the review intervals need to be much shorter than with slower moving industries such as engineering, construction, or staples.

Feedback may relate to a specific unit. At regular intervals, units should have their own retreat to deal with customer data coming in from all the tools (focus groups, surveys, and complaint systems). The flowdown from the CSS steering committee should be analyzed at the same time that any self-generated tools are considered. Looking at all the data simultaneously at regular points is vitally important for seeing the big picture and setting priority goals.

Wainwright has an exceedingly responsive customer satisfaction feedback mechanism. It measures satisfaction monthly. In the Mission Control Room at Wainwright, every key customer has a summary sheet on the wall. There is a red flag or a green flag by the name of the customer. If the satisfaction ratings fall below 95 percent, a red flag goes up. An owner is assigned to look for an immediate fix that will take care of the problem temporarily. If a longer-term fix is implied, a team goes to work.

Summary

This chapter on using CSS tools provides a glimpse at how to infuse passion into your CSS system. Converting data to spirited action is one of the biggest stumbling blocks of a CSS. Midas-touch deployment ignites the spirit behind continuous improvement through driving the system from the top; making it visible; defining owners, goals, and time frames; focusing on the positive; and properly channeling the data. Incentives for action work much better than beatings for not achieving goals. Part III (following) highlights how to analyze and synthesize data so that it is decision friendly for the strategic quality planning meeting.

Notes

1. Henry Bradshaw, CEO of Armstrong Building Products Operation, interview by author, Washington, D.C., 6 February 1996.

2. Robert Baer, CEO of United Van Lines, interview by author, Washington, D.C., 18 February 1996.

Part III

Data Analysis: Synthesis and Beyond

Going-for-the-Gold CSS: CSS Data Analysis

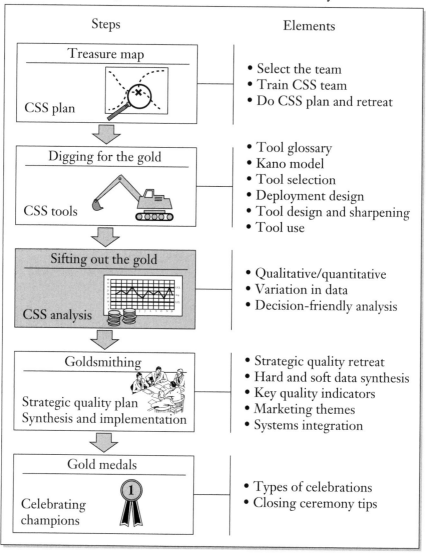

Steps   Elements

Treasure map

CSS plan

- Select the team
- Train CSS team
- Do CSS plan and retreat

Digging for the gold

CSS tools

- Tool glossary
- Kano model
- Tool selection
- Deployment design
- Tool design and sharpening
- Tool use

Sifting out the gold

CSS analysis

- Qualitative/quantitative
- Variation in data
- Decision-friendly analysis

Goldsmithing

Strategic quality plan
Synthesis and implementation

- Strategic quality retreat
- Hard and soft data synthesis
- Key quality indicators
- Marketing themes
- Systems integration

Gold medals

Celebrating
champions

- Types of celebrations
- Closing ceremony tips

Chapter 7

CSS Data Analysis: Sifting Out the Gold

This chapter highlights how to sort through all the dirt to sift out the gold. Sorting means distilling the information into the fewest common denominators. You will find two different sifting processes in this chapter: one on qualitative measures and one on quantitative. Qualitative measures (focus groups and interviews, win/loss analysis, and open-ended questions on surveys and observation) focus on in-depth understanding of clients and allow them to give free-form answers. Quantitative data deal with numbers that need to be compared and trended. Graphs are particularly useful for quantitative data. Dealing with both simultaneously allows for big-picture decisions.

Before you read this section, you will want to review the tool glossary near the back of the book and review any tools with which you are less familiar.

Qualitative vs. Quantitative Data

Open-ended questions, focus groups or interviews, advisory groups, and observation are all qualitative measures. Qualitative measures usually allow for more customer-driven, in-depth, subtle, or unconscious areas of customers' preferences to surface. Customers may have completely different words or ways of expressing their satisfiers and dissatisfiers than a researcher-driven survey methodology. Even though it is harder to roll-up this data, the input is vitally important to partnering with customers. These qualitative measures help the researcher do the following:

- Identify what is truly important to customers
- Identify unmet or latent needs
- Identify preferred features
- Identify how your product or service compares to your competitors'

You need qualitative measures to go beyond the superficial level. Many times questions are developed out of these qualitative measures and included in surveys over a broader sample. The soft aspect of qualitative measures refers to the perceptual nature of them. Customers' stated preferences and feelings are not always predictive of their buying behavior. They may say that certain features are important, yet still buy the cheapest product or service.

Quantitative data have numbers and can be averaged. Quantitative data give you scorecards, trend data, data that can be benchmarked, and other useful numbers.

Do not count just on quantitative measures. Why?

> *More than 80 percent of innovations in high-performing companies come from customers' ideas.*

Likewise, when I benchmarked both Baldrige Award winners and the Deming Prize winners in Japan, I found that 80 percent of the improvement team projects in these companies are driven from the top. The top, in these cases, means customers. Empowerment does not mean that the lowest-rank employees know intuitively what will cause customers to buy more products or services. It does mean that those frontline people should be polled to see what their collective day-by-day exposure to clients reveals (see observation tools in chapter 10). These observations should be part of the overall strategic quality planning where results from several tools are viewed simultaneously.

The deliverables of focus groups, focused interviews, and observations are hundreds of comments. Win/loss analyses can get the same result. When analyzed, you will find that these hundreds of comments can be boiled down to a vital few categories. You will want to boil the comments down through cluster analysis and reassign importance to the overall group through decibel analysis. A Pareto chart will summarize the two.

The primary ways of analyzing and synthesizing qualitative data are the following:

- Cluster analysis helps you determine the least number of categories.
- Decibel analysis helps you determine the emotional valence and loudness of the category.

Cluster Analysis

Boiling down massive amounts of free-form input can be a challenge. Exhibit 7.1 demonstrates how long lists of attributes can be condensed into features and given operational definitions.

- You actually start with attributes that are embedded in customer comments.

Feature	Attribute	Operational definition
Delivery	Timely	Within 20 minutes of promise
	Accurate	Has complete order
	Undamaged	Food is not damaged
	Clean	Trucks and drivers look clean
Invoices	Timely	Before 10th of month
	Accurate	Matches orders
	User-friendly	Follows customers' line items

Exhibit 7.1   Cluster analysis

- You perform a cluster analysis and cluster the attributes into features.

- Finally, you go back and get customer-desired specifics in your operational definition.

Information from focus groups, open-ended questions on surveys, focused interviews, and other qualitative measures can be synthesized by using cluster analysis. Have several researchers go over the notes and divide the customer satisfiers and dissatisfiers into major categories (features). You can group these easily with post-it notes and put all of the related items together. Then look for subgroups and determine the subgroup attribute clusters. If the probing has gone far enough, you should be able to pull out operational definitions. When a customer says the waiting line is short, the operational definition will specify exactly how long "short" is.

Directions for cluster analysis follow a three-step process.

1. Have one person go through all the comments and come up with no more than 10 basic requirements (they can have subsets).

2. Have three independent judges assign all of the individual comments to one of these requirements.

3. Do an interjudge reliability check to see if you have consistency among the judges (see reliability and validity in chapter 11).

Cluster analysis can be used to derive the key features, attributes, and operational definitions to use as a check sheet for complaint tracking systems. Customer service people end up with a check sheet in front of them that enables researchers to quantify the number of comments in any single line item.

Complaint Check Sheet and Decibel Analysis

Customer-driven or qualitative measures (see focus groups in chapter 10) can uncover expected customer requirements. You use quantitative written or telephone surveys to check both the importance of those requirements and satisfaction levels over a broader expanse of people.

In reducing all of the individual items to clusters, you lose the importance of the item to individual participants. Be sure to list the

Feature	Attribute	Total number	Decibel level of complaints		
			***	**	*
Delivery	On-time	51	32	17	2
	Accuracy	6	4	1	1
	Damaged	21	12	4	5

*** Very dissatisfied: probably won't buy again unless fixed

** Dissatisfied: may not buy again unless fixed

* Mildly dissatisfied: would like this area improved, but it is not critical

Exhibit 7.2   Complaint check sheet and decibel analysis.

number of comments that belong to each item. One way of coding decibel level is to have the researcher or customer service employee register a code by each tick on the list of typical complaint areas. This can either be done by hand or by computer tally. Instead of putting a tick in one column for each customer complaint feature and attribute, code the decibel level of the individual complaints for severity of the dissatisfaction. Exhibit 7.2 is an example of how the tabulation might look.

Opportunity Check Sheet

An opportunity check sheet can be developed for opportunities suggested directly or indirectly by customers. Some of these opportunities will be found in the customers' comments about your competitors' service or product. These opportunities eventually end up on your excited quality list to be considered in your strategic quality meeting. These features of your product or service would add that wow experience for customers.

Cluster analysis helps solidify an assortment of either positive or negative comments into categories that can be tracked. Complaint and opportunity check sheets with decibel analysis work well with any kind of frontline contact with customers. That includes repair, reservation agents, front-desk personnel, and cashiers. Likewise, the open-ended questions on telephone surveys and focus groups can be consolidated in this manner. (What did you like? What needs improvement?)

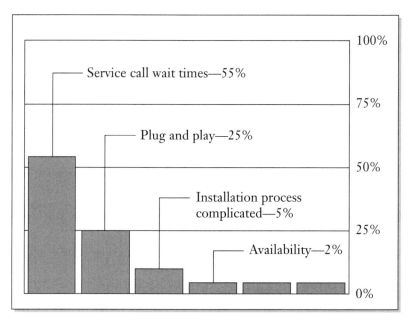

Exhibit 7.3   Complaint Pareto chart of a computer manufacturer.

The key categories can then be visually displayed on a Pareto chart. Pareto charts make it easy to separate out the vital few from the trivial many complaints or opportunities. Exhibit 7.3 shows that 85 percent of the complaints come from customers dissatisfied with service call wait times and plug-and-play capability (compatibility with other hardware and software).

Quantitative Measures

Survey scores and receipts (or bar code data) are the primary quantitative measure that you will use in the CSS. Many internal quality tools and market measures (number of defects, number of returned items, customer turnover rate, and market share) also represent hard data. Quantitative measures all use numbers.

You can have quantitative data in either soft or hard measures. Soft measures are those that measure perception and reactions. People may behave differently than what they say. Hard data are found at the cash register, in customer attrition rates, with market share, with revenues, and with profits. Quantitative and qualitative data are integrated at the strategic quality planning meeting for easy decision making.

Whether the numbers stem from quantitative questions in customer satisfaction surveys or client attrition, you still need to know what the numbers mean.

> *The problem with numbers is that, alone, they mean nothing.*

Comparative data are essential. Comparisons need to be made against your competition and against how you have performed in the past (trends).

For instance, you may receive a 95 percent on your customer satisfaction survey. As you are celebrating your success, your competitor, which received 98 percent, is busy stealing your market share. Over 24 time periods, you will end up with 17 percent market share in contrast to your competitor's 77 percent[1] (see chapter 1). Extensive research on 2746 business units with the PIMS database found three elements that are most predictive of overall growth and profit.[2]

1. Market share

2. Value (see value maps in chapter 10)

3. An overall satisfaction question on your survey

Thus, you need clear pictures of all three of these elements. You also need to be looking at these elements simultaneously with your CSS steering committee or executive committee. The pictures should include your competition and should be plotted over time. Examples of each are included in the next chapter on strategic quality planning.

Summary

Cluster analysis and decibel analysis are two ways to take qualitative material and reduce it to quantitative data. Showing the vital few compliments or complaints can be done in Pareto charts. Sources for these key issues are focus interviews and groups, open-ended questions, observation, and other open-ended measures. Dealing with qualitative material is vital to bringing the substantive voice of the customer into the organization. Hearing what customers have to say helps deepen the understanding of what really underlies their buying preferences.

Quantitative data can also be summarized to be more decision friendly. Bar charts, pie charts, and other graphics help make your quantitative data more easily understood. The tool tip section provides more illustrations of how to present decision-friendly data. The strategic quality planning meeting will provide examples of how to synthesize the data from the various sources.

Notes

1. Pete Babrich, "Customer Satisfaction: How Good Is Good Enough," *Quality Progress* 25, no. 12 (December 1992): 65–68.

2. Bradley T. Gale, *Managing Customer Value* (New York: Free Press, 1994), 301.

Going-for-the-Gold CSS: Strategic Quality Plan

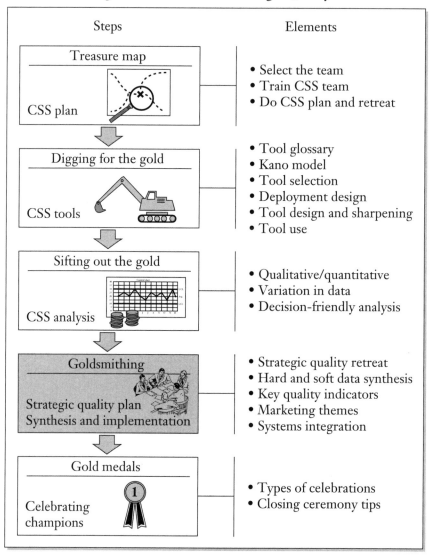

Steps	Elements
Treasure map — CSS plan	• Select the team • Train CSS team • Do CSS plan and retreat
Digging for the gold — CSS tools	• Tool glossary • Kano model • Tool selection • Deployment design • Tool design and sharpening • Tool use
Sifting out the gold — CSS analysis	• Qualitative/quantitative • Variation in data • Decision-friendly analysis
Goldsmithing — Strategic quality plan Synthesis and implementation	• Strategic quality retreat • Hard and soft data synthesis • Key quality indicators • Marketing themes • Systems integration
Gold medals — Celebrating champions	• Types of celebrations • Closing ceremony tips

Chapter 8

The Strategic Quality Planning Meeting: Goldsmithing

Looking at all the data simultaneously provides insights not available when looking at each piece at different times. Only when an integrated approach is used can a company extract the big picture. The big picture includes hard data like revenues, profits, market share, and employee and customer attrition. It also includes the voice of the customer in the soft data of complaints, lost customer reports, customer satisfaction data, and perceptual reports. Simplifying the presentation of complex data is helpful for executives and managers in making decisions.

The strategic quality meeting is where all of that information comes together. From looking at all the data simultaneously, it is easy to extract the strengths and weaknesses of the company. Those strengths are turned into areas to celebrate and market. The weaknesses become the improvement initiatives for the entire company or unit. This chapter walks you through this process.

Many times companies divide their strategic quality planning processes into two levels—long term and short term. The long-term plan is done at intervals of two to five years, depending upon how quickly the industry moves. The short-term plan is usually done at yearly intervals with quarterly checkups.

Preparation of the data is a key element of the strategic quality planning meeting. The facilitator usually outlines who needs to submit which data, what graphic representation (Pareto charts, line charts, and so on) need to be used, and what intervals of measurement are portrayed. These were already discussed in the CSS retreat at the beginning of the process. Who will correlate the data determined in the CSS retreat will also be confirmed. A statistician may want to conduct a regression analysis, for instance, on the relationship between revenues and customer satisfaction or between profits and attrition, and so on. The facilitator needs to receive these data at least two weeks ahead of the strategic planning retreat in order to integrate the information in a decision- and user-friendly package. That package can be distributed before the meeting so people have a chance to digest the information.

Elements of the strategic quality planning retreat are the following:

- Logistics
- The war room: hard and soft data synthesis
- Facilitation
- The customer satisfaction index
- Deployment of key quality objectives
- Marketing themes

Logistics

The strategic quality planning retreat typically takes two or three days, depending upon the size of the business. If the company is large, representatives from several product lines or units can be working in separate rooms and can come together at intervals to share notes. If the company is small or medium sized, the meeting is typically shorter (one or two days).

It is critical that the meeting be held off-site and without interruption. This is one of the most important meetings of the entire management structure. To take it lightly means that the executive level is not committed to quality. Likewise, using a facilitator for the meeting is imperative. This allows the manager and participants to deal with the content without having to run the meeting.

The War Room: Hard and Soft Data Synthesis

All of the data are posted on the walls around the room or on presentation boards at each table. One wall has hard data like revenue, profits, market share, and quality data. The other wall has customer satisfaction soft data such as customer satisfaction surveys, focus group cluster analysis, complaint tracking, and win/loss reports. Exhibits 8.1 and 8.2 show some of the data that can be displayed on the walls. Participants have received these charts well before the meeting.

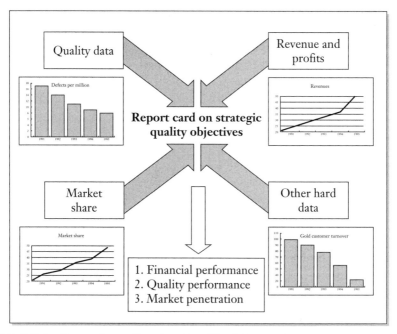

Exhibit 8.1   Strategic quality planning: Hard data review.

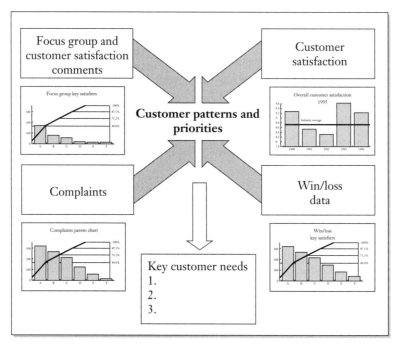

Exhibit 8.2   Strategic quality planning: Soft data review.

1. Assess target markets first. Order segments according to priority.
2. Review the hard (financial, attrition) data in chart form.
     Revenue and profits
     Market share and market share growth relative to competitors
     Quality and productivity measures (defects, inventory turnover rates)
     Customer and employee attrition rate charts
     Win/loss ratio
3. Review the soft (perceptual) data.
     Customer feature importance and satisfaction surveys (Pareto chart)
     Complaints (Pareto chart)
     Observations—dissatisfiers Pareto chart, satisfiers Pareto chart, other
        observations
     Win/loss reasons (Pareto chart)
     Reasons why customers and employees are leaving from lost customer
        research and exit interviews (Pareto chart)
4. Show data relationships (other relationships are also important).
     Employee vs. customer satisfaction and attrition
     Trends in revenues, profits, customer satisfaction, and market share
     Benchmark data—quality, revenues, and profits compared to
        competition
     Growth in revenue and profit vs. growth in customer satisfaction
     Satisfaction vs. market share growth
     Customer value map
5. Fill out feature importance and satisfaction chart.
     Place customer needs that are rated above and below average in the
        appropriate box
     Place high importance and high satisfaction needs in the key quality
        objectives box
     Place high importance and high satisfaction needs in the marketing
        themes box
6. Use the choosing key quality objectives chart to select goals.
7. (Optional) Develop an overall customer satisfaction index (see chapter 9).
8. Develop a celebration plan.

Exhibit 8.3   Strategic quality planning agenda.

When you are reviewing qualitative (soft) measures, keep in mind that customer satisfaction surveys and the value analysis are the two critical ingredients in your analysis. Complaints, win/losses, and observation are all reactive measures and may represent a small part of your customer base. Focus your energy accordingly.

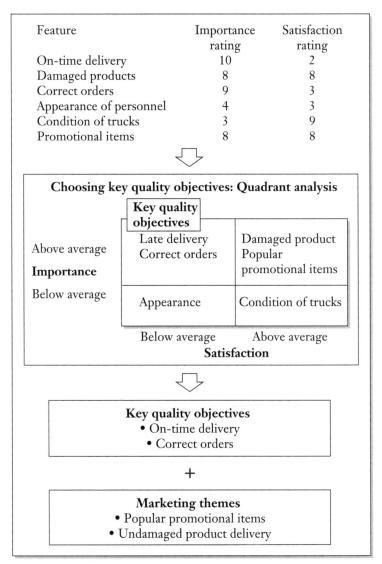

Feature	Importance rating	Satisfaction rating
On-time delivery	10	2
Damaged products	8	8
Correct orders	9	3
Appearance of personnel	4	3
Condition of trucks	3	9
Promotional items	8	8

Choosing key quality objectives: Quadrant analysis

	Key quality objectives	
Above average **Importance**	Late delivery Correct orders	Damaged product Popular promotional items
Below average	Appearance	Condition of trucks
	Below average	Above average
	Satisfaction	

Key quality objectives
- On-time delivery
- Correct orders

+

Marketing themes
- Popular promotional items
- Undamaged product delivery

Exhibit 8.4   Feature importance and satisfaction chart.

Exhibit 8.3, the strategic quality planning retreat agenda, highlights some of the topics that are typically covered in a retreat setting. Each of the topics is fully explained in the tool tip section.

Exhibit 8.4 illustrates one way of summarizing the importance ratings and satisfaction ratings of different features of a distribution company. From these two scores you can derive a quadrant analysis, which allows you to see what key quality objectives need to be set and what marketing messages to focus on.

The following points describe some of the other interesting things you can do with the data.

- *Correlate a key quality measure with revenue.* You can do this either by regression analysis or by visually comparing trends. Many managers don't understand regression analysis, so you might try a more manual way of making the same point. Make sure that your quality measure is tallied at the same interval (monthly, quarterly, and so on) and for the same time period as your revenue data. For instance, consider on-time deliveries: If this is a key need, a movement up or down in the line should predict upward or downward movement in revenue.

  Put the revenue trend line on a chart and make a transparency from it. Then have the managers slide the revenue transparency over the key quality trend line and see if there is a visual relationship between on-time delivery going up and revenue going up. Slide the transparency to the right and see if the lines are related, but just delayed by a few months. Usually you can see a relationship if it is a key quality need. This harks back to the point that improvements in EVA (including quality measures) lead to improvements in CVA, which finally lead to EVA (profits, revenue, market share).

- *Correlate employee attrition with customer attrition.* See if there is any relationship between losing employees and losing customers. In high-touch industries (hotels, airlines, advertising, and so on), this correlation is typically quite high.

- *Correlate the number of customers with growth in market share.* I have found with many businesses that the fewer total customers and the more target customers the business has, the greater their growth in overall market share. Less is more. That means focus has worked. We have usually been focusing on upselling gold customers as we diminish (without eliminating) the focus on selling to large quantities of small customers. Of course, if you have a product or service where repeat business or upselling is not an issue, this would not be true.

Facilitation

Good facilitation is just as important for the strategic quality planning meeting as it was for developing the CSS plan. This chapter cannot cover the nuances of how this process applies to your individual company. It depends on whether you have different locations, different product lines, and different ways of managing those product lines. The data presented would need to be tailored accordingly.

With different locations at the meeting, I usually present two levels in the meeting: location-based conclusions and overall company conclusions. Each location sits down with its own data and comes up with its location-based conclusions from a handful of strengths and weaknesses. You can easily take location-based data, post it on a presentation board as shown in Exhibit 8.5 and have participants discuss what they see.

Each location is given an assignment.

- Look at your revenue chart and mark the historical events, especially at the junctions. Historical events mean changes in management, quality indicators, new product launches, new competition, and so on.

- Look at the trends, levels, and variation in the data. What conclusions do you draw from this?

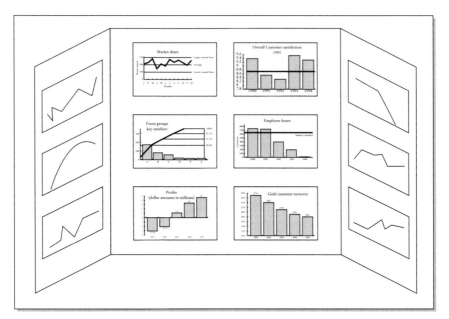

Exhibit 8.5   The presentation board.

- Based on the data, what would your customers say your strengths are (no more than four)?

- Based on the data, what would your customers say your weaknesses are (no more than four)?

Then all the locations come together for a look at companywide data. Charts with collective data for the entire company are used. Companywide conclusions result.

The Customer Satisfaction Index

An overall customer satisfaction index is used by some companies to consolidate diverse measures. The simplicity of one number is attractive. This step is not critical to success, because the index has to be uncoupled for corrective action anyway. If you have your hands full, skip this step.

The overall customer satisfaction index combines internal quality measures with value analysis and satisfaction ratings. This allows you to make comparisons over time across the complexity of data that are part of your customer assessment system. Assign weights to these scores *before* you look at all the data. Assigning weights afterward is subject to distortion because of the natural tendency to want to favor those areas that come out well. Better yet, have your customers assign weights. The component pieces are far more revealing than the overall customer satisfaction index. Still, companies find it helpful to have one simplified measure to see whether they are improving or losing ground overall.

Keep in mind that your priority scores are in four categories:

1. Customers—target segments, customer value map, attrition rates, lost customer Pareto, satisfaction

2. Financial and productivity—market share, revenues, productivity/employee, profit

3. Employees—employee satisfaction and attrition

4. Quality measures—on critical success factors derived from number 1

You may be asking how market share crept in. Isn't market share a by-product of all the good things a company does to satisfy its customers and keep its prices in check? Yes. It also has a magic all its own.

One commonly cited phenomenon in marketing is how companies "take off" when they reach 15 percent market share. The Japanese have known the secret for decades—they will go to great lengths to increase market share. The previously mentioned PIMS database of more than 2700 business units shows that merely achieving high market share—even if you didn't earn it—has enormous benefits, especially profitability.[1] In recent times competition has become so fierce that market share alone won't ensure success. Market-perceived quality is now a more important measure of competitiveness, according to Gale's research.[2]

A good part of market share is mind share—recognition of your company name at the point of purchase. The average person is exposed to 2500 marketing messages a day—through television, radio, billboards, newspapers, signs, flyers, catalogs, telephone solicitations, and so on. So much clutter exists that most people learn how *not* to let these messages register unless the message is relevant to them at the moment. Reaching a certain market share allows for a "clutter buster" reaction. Your company name appears before them more routinely, you may be discussed by your other customers, or the media may begin to pick up on you. Procter & Gamble spent more than $8.3 billion on marketing in the 1994–1995 fiscal year ending June 30, 1995.[3] That is why this formula also includes market share. If a product is the worst on the street at the highest prices but has 90 percent market share, somehow people (mistakenly) think the product is good. How could so many people be wrong?

Thus, the ultimate roll-up of all your internal and customer scores follows the model shown in Exhibit 8.6, the overall customer index. You may want to design your own. The supplier customer satisfaction index is a score that incorporates the quality measures you use to measure your suppliers.

Key processes are those critical success factors that you measure internally. For automotive parts, it may be defects per million. In hotels, it may be wait time for check in. For a software company, it may be the number of bugs per 1000 lines of code. These quality measures are precision measurements of those expected levels of quality.

Have key customers get involved in setting percentages in the right column that determine weights. That can be done with a representative sample of your key customer segment. Supplier percentages need to be determined internally, depending on how vital their parts are to your success. Doctors in a hospital are suppliers and may be

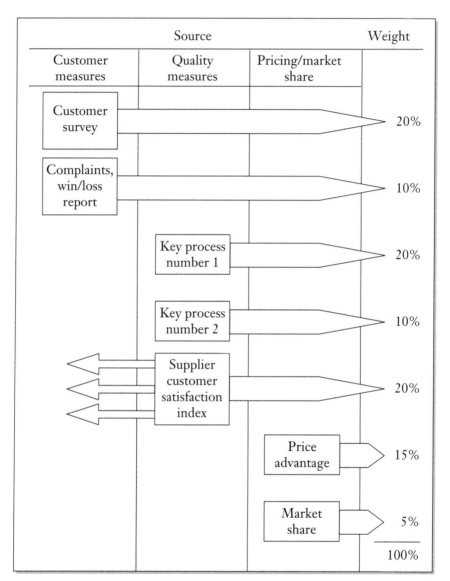

Exhibit 8.6   Overall customer index.

worth 75 percent on this chart. A pencil supplier wouldn't even be considered in the supplier measures of that same hospital. Reserve at least 5 percent for market share. The importance of market share diminished in the 1980s and early 1990s as companies like General Motors, IBM, and Eastern Airlines made it clear that you can't rest on your market share. Recent articles on brand equity (frequently generated by the large advertising budgets of those with high market share), say that it is coming back as a driver because consumers need a way to get through the clutter of too many choices.

David Aaker and Robert Jacobson found the same close relationship between 1000 customers' perceptions of brand quality and shareholder returns in a study of 34 companies.[4] They found the following:

> *Firms experiencing the largest gains in brand equity saw their stock return average 30 percent. Conversely, those firms with the largest losses in brand equity saw stock return average a negative 10 percent.*

This overall customer index is a useful tool for looking at an overall trend line. The industry average can be derived only if your competitors are included in the same model as you (see Exhibit 8.7). As was mentioned before, companies like J.D. Powers have one model that includes Japanese and American auto companies. Hotels have overall rating services like Mobil and AAA.

An overall customer index should correlate to increases in revenue over a long period of time. It does not predict sudden technical leaps, sharp regulatory shifts, or outside influences that are not under the control of the company. These shifts should be on the radar scope and should influence a "thinking-out-of-the-box" portion of the strategic

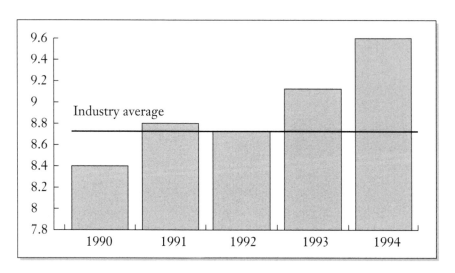

Exhibit 8.7   Customer satisfaction compared to industry average.

quality planning meeting. That thinking-out-of-the-box element is probably best done at a separate time in a new product development meeting when people are not bogged down in data and decisions.

Deployment of Key Quality Objectives

A customer-focused organization is driven by the rolled-up feedback from this system. Now that you have your vital few key quality objectives, you need to be interlocked in spirit, in mind, and in the goals of the entire organization.

- Have the CEO perform a strategic quality objectives launch. As with any product or service launch, it takes energy and credibility to get the attention of overworked employees. High-performing companies like Coca-Cola, Procter & Gamble, McDonald's, and Microsoft know the importance of first selling and training employees on a new service or product before going to customers. Major changes in processes can also use this spurt of energy. The CSS is definitely deserving.

- Take your objectives and have each unit look at its own process maps—the steps by which the different deliverables get done. Ordering, writing contracts, procurement, shipping, and manufacturing each have processes. Identify which processes and subprocesses relate to the strategic quality initiatives.

- Select a quality improvement team (QIT) or an individual to own each process improvement. Make sure each has an executive sponsor.

- Have each QIT identify performance gaps between what the performance is now and where it needs to be.

- Benchmark internally or externally to identify what goals are realistic. Use historical data to set goals.

- Use positive rewards and contests to help motivate the QITs.

- Determine the QIT project plan and review process.

Johnson & Johnson has used this process to link external customer drivers to internal measures. "Unless your measures interlock, you don't have a customer-driven system and can end up wasting resources on improving processes that mean little to customers."[5]

Marketing Themes

In addition to the honest self-assessment that is an integral part of a going-for-the-gold customer assessment system, you can capitalize on this analysis in your marketing efforts.

In a telephone survey of 392 senior marketing executives, exactly half told *The Marketing Report* staff that sales call reports are not used by marketing.[6] Frontline employees and salespeople are some of the best sources of marketing intelligence. Using more frontline information was helpful in the sales bidding success rate jumping from 23 percent to 76 percent at Flour Daniel. It is vitally important that the customer satisfaction measurement system include a systematic way to gather these data and fold them into strategic quality planning and marketing.

Take the chart you developed on key quality objectives and now look at your target marketing theme areas (see Exhibit 8.8). While you quietly work on those improvement areas, you advertise your strengths. Marketing themes are drawn from what is important to customers and the areas in which they rated you as best in class.

Procter & Gamble learned this lesson the hard way. It found that four-fifths of its advertising was not effective.[7] Its root cause analysis found that the one-fourth that was effective happened to emphasize the features that customers had reported as important in customer research.

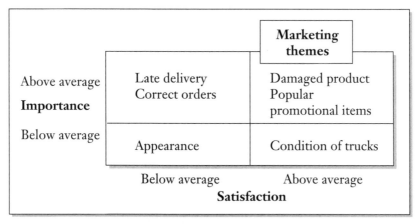

Exhibit 8.8   Choosing marketing themes.

Procter & Gamble's prior policy was that consumer research was highly proprietary. These secret data did not get communicated to the advertising agency that designed the strategy for an ad campaign. So the ad agency was left to guess what was important. Changing the policies for Procter & Gamble optimized its advertising dollars.

The campaigns that captured customer preferences for simplicity, price, emotional appeal, and loyalty stopped a steady exodus of customers from AT&T that had lasted for 11 years. Its cost of obtaining customers decreased by $3 per person compared to 1993.[8] This is a good example of integrating research, strategy, value analysis, and profits!

The beauty of this going-for-the-gold model is that the message in the advertising matches the customer's experience. You thus use advertising to reinforce the positive perceptions with existing customers and possibly expand positive word of mouth.

Companies that proclaim slogans not based on the real experience of customers just give customers more cause to expand their negative word of mouth. Holiday Inn's "no surprises" advertising message causes us to expect consistency. Has "no surprises" been your experience at Holiday Inn? This was such a big issue that Holiday Inn delivered an edict to its 800 aging hotels that they will meet new specifications to ensure consistency by 1997 or lose their franchise.[9] United Airlines creates an expectation that the skies are going to be friendly. Are they? Advertising should make people feel good about a company, not remind them of negative experiences. Don't let your advertising agency just glibly write creative copy without addressing the real needs revealed through customer satisfaction and perception measures.

The integration of customer needs assessment, satisfaction measures, and marketing cannot be overemphasized. In global competition, most technical companies are feeling the "need for speed." Hewlett-Packard products developed within the last two years accounted for two-thirds of its revenue in 1993.[10]

How Much Advertising?

Just as market share is a powerful driver, so is effective advertising. The PIMS database mentioned previously also studied the relationship between advertising relative to competitors. In this research, brands that spent a larger-than-average share of their sales on advertising earned an average return on investment of 32 percent.[11] Brands that advertised less than competitors earned only 17 percent. That is a tremendous discriminator for a large number of companies

(2746). Another survey of 500 companies found that companies having higher ratios of marketers to engineers had larger market shares and were faster to market with new products. Whether companies are using marketing to provide customer input to engineers or using it to talk to customers about improvements, both are vital to success.[12]

Thus, perceived improvements in product quality is highly correlated with large market share. AT&T found a three-month delay in these two figures. Those companies that both improve perceived quality and have larger than their competitors' advertising expenditures "earn much more than companies that spend less."[13] (Hopefully your competitors are not reading this same book.)

Advertising is so powerful—Gale found that increases in advertising expenditures were closely correlated with market share gains,[14] even after adjusting for changes in

- Sales promotions
- New product introductions
- Relative quality improvements
- Growth of the served markets
- Changes in spending on the company sales force

Procter & Gamble's introduction of Aleve, a painkiller, was a good example of what advertising can do. In a market with more than 150 aspirin and painkiller products, Aleve stole a 6.5 percent monthly share of a $2.6 million analgesic market in August 1994. That put it in the number three spot overnight. Procter & Gamble spent $100 million to launch it, and recognized that analgesic users are sophisticated. The ads feature 12-hour relief with the tag line, "All day long. All day strong."[15]

Advertise your successes.

How do you know how much your competitors are spending? Most large companies like Coca-Cola, PepsiCo, and the like require that advertising agencies give them "comps" that tell them what their competitors are spending at the local level. *Advertising Age* also publishes comparative spending rates at regular intervals. Otherwise, you can have the same outside firm that conducts your benchmark survey collect and disseminate that data. Most successful companies have realized the benefit of cooperating with their competitors to get comparative data.

Systems Integration

Systems integration involves tying key quality objectives into everyday work life. Key quality objectives turn into overall company or division initiatives. In Exhibit 8.5 these quality objectives included accurate invoicing and better delivery. Each department then spends some time coming up with aspects of what they do that affects the overall goals to meet the initiatives. Those goals would cascade down to individuals, who would have them written into their performance appraisal goals. Tying bonus programs to meeting goals on key quality initiatives is especially powerful for turning initiatives into action.

Unless the strategic quality objectives are tied to the ongoing systems of the organization, they are likely not to be implemented over time. Those systems include compensation bonuses, hiring criteria, promotion criteria, and performance appraisals. If the only thing employees hear about the strategic quality goal is what metric will be used, they will dutifully take the data and not bother to try to improve.

Make the strategic quality goals visible to employees at every turn. When posting a job promotion announcement on a bulletin board, relate the promotion to how the person contributed to the strategic quality goals. Put the strategic quality goals in recruitment ads and brochures. Strategic quality goals should be translated into specific behaviors that appear in performance appraisals. Everyone in the company—from the CEO to the janitors—should have bonuses contingent on the achievement of companywide strategic quality objectives.

The Government Accounting Office concurs with these points. Baldrige Award finalists that have formal quality programs with compensation, training, hiring, and promotion tied to customer satisfaction and quality performance scores were significantly better in profits, market share, and customer satisfaction than were their lesser-ranked counterparts.

At Prism, for instance, advertisers said they wanted results from radio advertising. Prism had plenty of success stories in which radio advertising had delivered incredible results. First we had to analyze what made those campaigns successful. The elements included proper client needs assessment, good strategic analysis, good creative concept, and efficiency measures (how much advertising worked and what times of the day it worked best). All of this research and creativity was folded into an integrated marketing campaign. Then we packaged these elements of integrated marketing campaigns into a getting-results training program and trained the best salespeople. We then tracked the results that the advertisers achieved. Thus, training became client driven. As a result of increased results enjoyed by advertisers, Prism tripled its cash flow in less than three years.

Hiring is yet another systems element that is influenced by the key quality objectives and the marketing theme. Look for people with strengths in those areas deemed important to customers. If creativity is important to customers, stress creativity in relevant positions. If teamwork is important, stress teamwork in customer contact positions.

Summary

The strategic quality planning meeting is a good place to synthesize the data—both hard data from revenues, profits, market share, and attrition, as well as soft data from perceptual measures. If done well, participants can both gain insights into what caused changes in trends and distill their key quality objectives and marketing themes. Focus is the key. The company or division usually has its hands full with three or four of each. Deploying those will be hard enough. Each department or team can add unique improvement areas. The strategic quality planning group is looking for key initiatives on major issues, not nits.

It is important to embed the objectives and marketing themes into your bonus plan, performance appraisal system, hiring, and training.

Notes

1. Bradley T. Gale, *Managing Customer Value* (New York: Free Press, 1994), 166.
2. Ibid., 167.
3. Anne R. Carrey, "P&G Ad Cuts?" *USA Today*, 19 February 1996, B6.
4. David Aaker and Robert Jacobson, "Study Shows Brand-Building Pays Off for Stockholders," *Advertising Age*, 18 July 1994, 18.

5. Susan Lemons, vice president of quality management and reengineering at Johnson & Johnson, "Successful Reengineering Starts with the Customer" (speech given at the 8th Annual Customer Satisfaction Conference, Washington, D.C., 18–20 February 1995).

6. George Walther, "Customer Contact: Small Investment, Big Payoff," *The Marketing Report*, 23 January 1995, 2.

7. W. Edwards Deming, "Plan for Action for the Optimization of Service Organizations" (speech given at the Optimization of Service Organizations Conference, San Jose, California, 21–22 July 1992).

8. "AT&T Ads Cut Confusion," *USA Today*, 15 December 1994, 3B.

9. E. Jones, "Holiday Inns to Spruce Up or Check Out," *USA Today*, 14 September 1994, B1.

10. "HP's Platt Lauded," *Industry Week*, 19 December 1994, 30.

11. Gale, *Managing Customer Value*, 160.

12. Jon Brecka, "Good News for Marketers! Survey Says Hire More Marketing Staff," *Quality Progress* 27, no. 12 (December 1994): 16.

13. Gale, *Managing Customer Value*, 162.

14. Ibid., 163.

15. "P&G's Aleve Quickly Joins Top Painkillers," *Advertising Age*, 7 December 1994, 3.

Going-for-the Gold CSS: Celebrating Champions

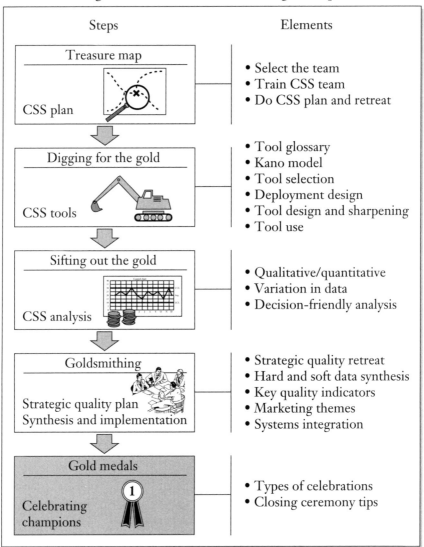

Steps	Elements
Treasure map CSS plan	• Select the team • Train CSS team • Do CSS plan and retreat
Digging for the gold CSS tools	• Tool glossary • Kano model • Tool selection • Deployment design • Tool design and sharpening • Tool use
Sifting out the gold CSS analysis	• Qualitative/quantitative • Variation in data • Decision-friendly analysis
Goldsmithing Strategic quality plan Synthesis and implementation	• Strategic quality retreat • Hard and soft data synthesis • Key quality indicators • Marketing themes • Systems integration
Gold medals Celebrating champions	• Types of celebrations • Closing ceremony tips

Chapter 9

Celebrating Champions: Gold Medals

Another vital (and yet often overlooked) part of your CSS is celebrating the team, division, or individual successes that helped you achieve better or stellar scores. This chapter highlights the types of celebrations you can arrange, provides ideas, and finishes with closing ceremonies.

Types of Celebrations

Sideline Celebrations

The high-fives in the hall from respected managers are powerful. Starting each meeting with recent accomplishments is highly motivating to people. Build celebration into the everyday workplace. Little ceremonies and creative contests can ultimately be worth more than larger award ceremonies that are held infrequently. As a side note, one way to see which companies have gold CSS is to stop at the local trophy stores. In the more than 25 cities where I checked, I noticed a strong association between high-performing companies with gold customer satisfaction systems and those that do the most business with trophy stores. Interesting, but not scientific.

Ideas are listed in Exhibit 9.1 for these sideline celebrations. The best ideas often come from employees. Use this list just to trigger your imagination.

Rewards

1. Training for an individual or team (very popular in Japan)

2. Trips to showcase improvements (Team Expo at Armstrong BPO)

3. Extra days off (Castle Rock Military Base, Zytec)

4. Qualify to enter drawing for big prize (United Van Lines, Prism)

5. Menu-driven rewards, point system determines selection (Microsoft)

6. Auctions for gifts based on point accumulations (Prism)

Recognition

1. Employee success features on television, print, or radio ads (Hawaii Hilton)

2. Advertisements of winning salespeople (Merrill Lynch)

3. Hero team awards posted on bulletin boards (most Baldrige Award winners)

4. Atta-boys (or girls) from the CEO (Fluor Daniel)

5. Lunch out with the CEO, executive slaves for a day (Prism)

6. Poster blowups of teams or individuals with captions (dozens of companies)

7. Visible symbols of accomplishment (special watches or paper-weights)

Exhibit 9.1   Reward and recognition ideas.

Customer Celebrations

Customers need to be notified of what was done with their suggestions. This will motivate them to be part of your system in the future. Thank-you notes after customers participate in a survey or focus group are a must.

Customers are also interested in what changes happened as a result of their participation. Eastman Chemical, which surveys its 14,000 customers every other year and has about an 80 percent return rate, found that educating customers about changes was a vital part of building partnerships and actually increased ratings during the next survey. Don't advertise, though, unless your improvements are solid and stable. Otherwise you are not managing expectations honestly.

Closing Ceremonies

At least once a year, companies of all sizes need to hold companywide (or unit-wide) celebrations. Lots of companies have social celebrations but really miss the opportunity to recognize employees in front of spouses and friends. The other mistake is to do this only for the sales force. It typically receives a disproportionate amount of credit for success (or failure) than it deserves. An irresistible product or service doesn't take much selling. That's where the gold is.

Some tips for closing ceremonies follow:

- Give as many team rewards as you can.
- Get customers to give some of the speeches.
- Put some imagination and creativity into the awards
- Budget for celebration.
- Focus on the whole organization—not just sales or the top level.
- Give more awards rather than fewer.
- Include awards for effort as well as for improvements with high financial returns.
- Insert fun throughout.

The Next Morning

So what happens now that the data are all analyzed, synthesized, and embedded in the strategic quality, marketing, and business plan (at Armstrong these are all the same—good idea). The review processes were discussed. The systems issues like hiring, training, and so on have been tied in. Celebrations help make it fun.

It's important to make the system positive beyond the celebration. The strategic improvement initiatives cascade down through the division goals, the unit goals, and the individual performance goals. All are monitored at predefined intervals. Tying these goals to salary bonuses works well. Continuous points of recognition for goals accomplished early or well keeps the fires lit.

Periodic review of the customer satisfaction measurement system is important. Central issues include the following:

- How to tighten the cycle time from input to decision making
- How to heighten buy-in of the people making changes
- How to make measurement fun instead of a chore
- How to better communicate results to customers, managers, and employees
- How to pick the right promoters of your CSS
- Others?

Usually lots of "other" ideas emerge from the mere act of having the CSS steering committee members poll their departments for feedback on how to improve the system. Likewise, customers need to be asked how the data gathering and communication with them might be improved.

Tools that don't seem to have short-term or long-term return on investment should be discarded. A company with very low customer turnover (less than 5 percent) may want to spread out the intervals of measurement or drop lost customer surveys altogether.

Motivating Employees over the Long Term

While in Japan, I was particularly intrigued with how to keep service and product quality alive over decades. Many of the companies I work with start to worry after five years. Most companies go through a pattern of moving forward and stalling, moving forward and stalling. Moving over the speed bumps takes commitment from the top. Creativity is imperative. Many Japanese companies have major competitions among their units to drive energy. They have lots of recognition and status associated with winning. Keeping people constantly informed of those competitors that are creeping up on you also helps.

Summary

This chapter focused on how to ignite the spirit behind a gold customer measurement and management system. Focusing on the positive in celebrations through special recognition ceremonies, bonuses, opportunities for visibility before executives, and the improvement issues by addressing systems changes will help you drive change. Hiring, promotions, compensation, training, departmental goal setting, and performance appraisals all need to link to the key target markets, the strategic quality initiatives, and the marketing features that surface from measuring and managing the CSS.

Part IV

Tool Tip Section

Chapter 10

Tools for Gathering Data

Advisory Groups

Definition

Advisory groups are volunteer groups of customers that meet at regular intervals to provide in-depth suggestions and direction to a company. Sometimes community or industry leaders or experts are also included. Some of the purposes advisory groups serve are to:

- Provide ideas for technical or service innovations
- Detail dissatisfiers
- Provide network opportunities or access that may not otherwise be available
- Test products or services
- Represent a wide range of input
- Be ambassadors for the company

Benefits

Advisory groups provide an opportunity for valued customers to co-develop your product or service. Delta Airlines started 10 business advisory groups around the country in 1994, using them to refine services for its frequent business flyers. Suggestions ranged from improving the baggage compartments of Lockheed 1011 airplanes to offering more variety in meal service.

Advisory groups offer the same opportunities to probe as focus groups. Advisory groups also set up partnerships with valued customers. The more they invest in your company, the more likely it is that they will be ambassadors to sell your company to others (especially if you listen to them).

How?

1. First, set objectives for the advisory board. Be honest. If you want the board members to help you connect to the outside world, select members and construct the agenda in that direction. If you want them to help you refine services or products, the selection process and agenda will be entirely different.

2. Advisory boards can meet anywhere from monthly to quarterly to semiannually. Semiannually is less demanding on the board members, but doesn't allow you to keep up with your dynamic competition.

3. Use a trained facilitator. A facilitator will help draw out quiet participants, keep the meeting on track, and record comments without bias.

4. Train the representatives from the company to respond in a neutral manner. Having company representatives defend their positions or sell to the advisory board will sabotage the purpose and decrease honesty.

5. Acknowledge the status of your advisory board members by giving them adequate notice about meetings, asking when is the best meeting time for them, and treating their opinions with respect.

6. Symbols of participation can be special badges of honor. Delta Airlines gave us special business advisory notepaper, a desk model of a Delta 767, and free tickets to the Rose Bowl. These symbols helped etch our loyalty more deeply.

7. At each meeting, summarize the changes that have been made and discuss why other changes were not made.

8. Circulate the agenda in advance.

Who?

Advisory board members are selected based on your objectives. If your objectives focus on service or product feedback and improvements, make sure you have adequate representation from market segments that are important to you. For example, the following segments are important for an airline advisory group.

- The high-profit customer base (frequent business travelers)
- Representative industries (travel agents and business travelers)
- Representative uses of the product (international, short haul, and long haul)
- Representative geographies

If possible, select out those members with personalities that are likely to dominate or intimidate others. Known personality conflicts and sensitive competitors should also be avoided.

Complaint Tracking

Definition

Many companies have 800 numbers for customers to call and express their complaints and compliments. An IBM study showed that, for every dissatisfied customer that complains, nine others just leave. Every dissatisfied customer may tell 10 other people. Thus, a single complaint may represent 100 potentially lost customers. Thus, resolving each complaint represents an opportunity to retain 100 customers.

Examples

Hewlett-Packard assigns an owner to every suggestion or complaint that comes into the company. Standards for resolution have been set. A companywide database alerts the owner when the complaint has not been resolved.

Federal Express has the standard, "Never let the sun set on a complaint." In other words, the person complaining will at least be sent a written progress report that day.

Deployment

Wainwright prides itself on its highly responsive complaint handling. The person receiving the complaint gives an immediate response with what will happen. The complaint form goes through the distribution process and is signed by the CEO and the plant manager before moving on to the group leaders. It is also tracked in a database. All complaints are handled this way. The customer champion is in charge of the complaint resolution process. If a red flag is up beside the customer's picture in the war room, everyone makes a considerable effort to get it down. An action plan has to be developed within 24 hours for how to turn that flag green.

Tracking

Software programs can be custom designed to track each complaint. These programs can be used to set alarms when the resolution takes longer than the standard time. Cycle-time reduction is an important aspect of complaint handling. The Lotus Notes software program offers a helpful way to note customer complaints, standardize the way in which they are collected, and make the data instantly available to process owners.

Customer Satisfaction Surveys

What Are Customer Satisfaction Surveys?

Customer satisfaction surveys are written questionnaires that determine levels of satisfaction with various facets of the product or service. Surveys are one of the *most abused* quality tools. Many organizations quickly compose a superficial set of questions and then send it to a sampling of customers. Then these organizations base their entire quality strategies on a return rate of less than 15 percent for their questionnaires. The questions frequently don't represent what is important to customers, and the answers are from too small a sample size.

The better example discussed earlier was Eastman Chemical, a 1993 Baldrige Award winner. It thoroughly tested its survey before sending it out. Its commitment to the results is evident in the way the survey is deployed. Salespeople hand-deliver the surveys to more than 14,000 customers worldwide. The customers return the surveys to a neutral internal party. Customers are called if the survey is not returned in a set amount of time. The return rate is more than 80 percent. The salesperson then follows up with each customer to review the overall results and what is being done in each area indicated for correction.

Benefits

Surveys can provide a way to compare key quality indicators from year to year. They provide important information about the perception of your quality or service. If done well, they can also show how you rate compared to your competition.

Tips on Customer Satisfaction Surveys

Sample.   Samples need to be statistically representative of your customer base. You might want to stratify your customer base into categories. A tax software company, for example, might have the following categories.

Frequency of use: Frequent user, infrequent user, nonuser

Categories of use: Accountants, bookkeepers, end users

Demographics: Geography, age, income, and so on

Then randomly sample from within those subsets.

Bias.   Biased questions that reflect what you want to hear won't provide much insight. The National Rifle Association sent out a questionnaire that asked, "Do you think your constitutional rights should be violated?" A waiter at a restaurant asks, "Do you want me to pass on any compliments to the chef?"
    Bias can be difficult to detect when reviewing your own work. Have someone else double-check your questions to make sure they are unbiased.

Ambiguity.   Questions with ambiguity are interpreted differently by different people. One popular ambiguous question is, "How would you rate the professionalism of our staff?" Does professionalism mean how well staff members are dressed? How quickly staff members responded? How accurate their answers were? Again, giving people an opportunity to discuss the meaning of your questions will help you avoid ambiguous ones.

User Friendly.   A user-unfriendly survey is long and looks as if it will take more than three minutes to fill out. Lots of open-ended questions are a turn-off. A user-friendly survey is simple, easy to complete, and easily folded to put in the return mail. Two pages is the maximum length. Large postcards are ideal. Watch for visual clutter. If the survey is not user-friendly, you initiate a bias in those who return the survey. Only the highly committed will bother. Longer surveys are only appropriate for high-relationship customers (professional organizations, distributors, business-to-business customers, and so on).

Simplicity.   A complex question asks several things at the same time. Asking people to agree or disagree with a statement such as "Our staff was both fast and friendly" will cause confusion.

Frequency of Measuring Customer Satisfaction

A yearly interval is maximum. Beyond a year, people don't remember their experiences or feelings or they may have moved. If you are going to measure at more frequent intervals than quarterly, use a more personal approach. Customers typically don't like to fill out forms.

Steps in Measuring Customer Satisfaction

A logical order is helpful in designing any survey used in measuring customer satisfaction. Exhibit 10.1 portrays these steps.

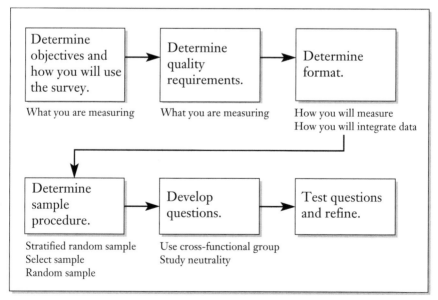

Exhibit 10.1   Steps in customer survey design.

How to Formulate Questions

You have several choices in how to format questions. The following are the most popular.

Yes/no questions

Was the food served warm?	❐ Yes ❐ No
Were the answers accurate?	❐ Yes ❐ No

Likert scale questions (the most popular scale used)
The food was served warm.
   ❐ Strongly agree ❐ Agree ❐ So-so ❐ Disagree ❐ Strongly disagree

The answers were accurate.
   ❐ Strongly agree ❐ Agree ❐ So-so ❐ Disagree ❐ Strongly disagree

   The five-point Likert scale offers more accurate calibration of the answers. Having more than five points does not necessarily increase accuracy.

Expectations vs. Results Questions.   As indicated previously, service quality amounts to results minus expectations. Thus, you need to know what people expect of your service or product to know what their rating really means. The example of a customer satisfaction form given at the end of this section illustrates that format.

Overall Measures of Satisfaction.   Include at least one question about overall satisfaction in your survey. Following are some examples.

What was your overall level of satisfaction with this service/product?
   ❐ Excellent ❐ Very good ❐ So-so ❐ Dissatisfied ❐ Strongly dissatisfied

I would use the service/product again.
   ❐ Strongly agree ❐ Agree ❐ So-so ❐ Disagree ❐ Strongly disagree

I would recommend this service/product to others.
   ❐ Strongly agree ❐ Agree ❐ So-so ❐ Disagree ❐ Strongly disagree

   As John Newbold, director of market research at Compaq said about Compaq's system, using a composite of all three measures is more robust than just one. Overall satisfaction by itself does not embrace the whole picture.[1]

The first question about overall satisfaction offers the highest prediction of whether customers will buy your service or product again. Pay particular attention to the answers to this question.

Put the overall measures of satisfaction at the beginning of your survey. Overall satisfaction answers become distorted if preceded by lists of questions that begin to shape a person's thinking.

Length of Survey

Base the length of your survey on the relationship with the customer and when the survey is done. High-relationship customers depend on your products or services for their success, so they typically *want* to give more feedback. Engineers surveyed by the Society for Mechanical Engineers gave higher response rates for an eight-page survey than a four-page survey. One hospital I worked with had a 100 percent response rate with a 12-page questionnaire, but only because an interviewer conducted the survey at bedside and the patients wanted a distraction. Frequent flyers in first class are a captive audience. A longer questionnaire would be much more appropriate in that setting than sending a questionnaire to a busy executive's office. If you are sending a survey to low-relationship clients, two user-friendly pages is about the longest you want to aim for.

Only a few companies have done research on return rates with various lengths of surveys. Their research supports these conclusions. Remember that, if you want lots of information, consider a more personal contact through a telephone or personal interview. A low response rate (anything less than 50 percent) distorts the ability you have to make decisions from such a small sampling of your customer base. A higher response rate is more critical than are a couple more pages.

How to Tabulate and Show Results

Organizations can take the easy approach and just tabulate the percentage of people who responded favorably. Thus, the results might be shown in a graph similar to Exhibit 10.2.

Further Tips on Surveys

1. Pilot your survey with representative customers to make sure that you have included the key questions and that the questions are clearly and neutrally worded.

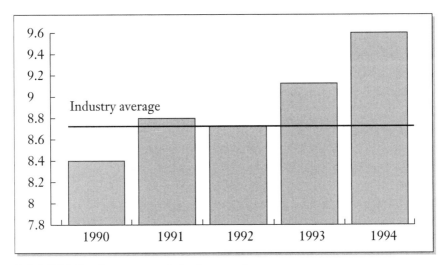

Exhibit 10.2   Customer satisfaction graph.

2. Be proactive about your surveys. Instead of sending them by mail, ask customers to fill them out before leaving your establishment. Create an incentive system for employees to have customers fill out the surveys. You can double your response rate just by having employees ask your customers to fill out the survey and then asking customers if they have done so.

3. If you do mail the survey, include a motivating paragraph or letter. You need to encourage people to take the time and trouble to fill out the survey and send it in. Ways you can motivate people to complete the survey include the following:

   a. Tell customers how you will use the information to enhance your service to them.

   b. Let customers know their reactions are an important part of determining where you spend your improvement dollars.

   c. Add an incentive for returning the form. Incentives that work are extra frequent flyer points, a coupon for merchandise, or a chance at a drawing.

4. Ask for qualifying information. Questions should help you determine whether the person is a frequent customer or someone who has never used your services.

5. Ask questions about your competition (if you have room). This will give you good comparative data.

6. Leave room for comments. You might want two categories, such as what customers like and what suggestions they have for improvements.

7. Leave space for them to sign their names and write their phone numbers. Specify that this information is optional. You then have a chance to call those people who responded in very positive or negative directions.

Sample Customer Satisfaction Questionnaires

The questionnaire in Exhibit 10.3 is meant to be an illustration of a SERVQUAL-type survey, not one that can be lifted from this book and used on your customers. These questions are generic to service. Your questions need to be specific to your service or product. Likewise, you could be missing some vital questions that are critical to the buying behaviors of your customers. Thus, go through the extra step of finding out what questions *your customers* want to be asked. The problem with the questionnaire in Exhibit 10.3 is that you normally hear that almost everything is important. A better way to refine your understanding of importance is to ask the questions in a way that forces answers and helps you weight your responses. Exhibit 10.4, from a distribution company, is a better example of clustering questions, finding some customer perceptions of competitors, and looking at importance issues. Survey questions should help you insert operational definitions for each of the categories. Operational definitions can be determined as in the following example:

> The expectation for on-time delivery means the delivery arrives within what interval of the time from when it was promised?
>
> ❐ 10 minutes ❐ 30 minutes ❐ 60 minutes ❐ 2 hours ❐ 4 hours

If your calculations show that there is a wide gap between what your customer expects and what you deliver, you need further research. Focused interviews with key customers could help you understand what price they would be willing to pay for more precise delivery times.

Another good question is, "What would it take to get you to shift your business from Company X to us?" This question would be followed by probing.

Customer surveys need to be customized for market segments, with a few common questions. The key common questions relate to overall satisfaction—will they buy again and would they refer someone

When was the last time you used this service or product? _____

How often have you used this service/product? At least:
❏ Once a day ❏ Once a week ❏ Once a month ❏ Once a year ❏ Never

What competitor products or services do you typically use? _____

Overall level of satisfaction:
1. What was your overall level of satisfaction with this service/product?
   ❏ Excellent ❏ Very good ❏ So-so ❏ Dissatisfied ❏ Strongly Dissatisfied
2. I would use the service/product again.
   ❏ Strongly Agree ❏ Agree ❏ So-so ❏ Disagree ❏ Strongly Disagree
3. I would recommend this service/product to others.
   ❏ Strongly Agree ❏ Agree ❏ So-so ❏ Disagree ❏ Strongly Disagree

Circle the number that best represents your feelings. The first set of numbers relates to your expectations, the second to how the company performed.

		Degree of importance to me (1 = unimportant, 5 = very important)					Degree of excellence that company X does this (1 = does not occur, 5 = always occurs)				
1.	Facilities are clean.	1	2	3	4	5	1	2	3	4	5
2.	Employees are neat in appearance.	1	2	3	4	5	1	2	3	4	5
3.	Employees respond in a timely manner.	1	2	3	4	5	1	2	3	4	5
4.	Invoices are easy to understand.	1	2	3	4	5	1	2	3	4	5
5.	Answers to questions are accurate.	1	2	3	4	5	1	2	3	4	5
6.	Employees are courteous.	1	2	3	4	5	1	2	3	4	5
7.	Problem solving is customer oriented.	1	2	3	4	5	1	2	3	4	5
8.	Operating hours are convenient.	1	2	3	4	5	1	2	3	4	5
9.	Manuals are easy to follow.	1	2	3	4	5	1	2	3	4	5
10.	Customers receive personal attention.	1	2	3	4	5	1	2	3	4	5
11.	Safety is emphasized.	1	2	3	4	5	1	2	3	4	5
12.	Employees understand my needs.	1	2	3	4	5	1	2	3	4	5
13.	The service is prompt.	1	2	3	4	5	1	2	3	4	5
14.	Deadlines are met.	1	2	3	4	5	1	2	3	4	5
15.	The product is easy to use.	1	2	3	4	5	1	2	3	4	5
16.	The product is reliable.	1	2	3	4	5	1	2	3	4	5
17.	The price is reasonable.	1	2	3	4	5	1	2	3	4	5
18.	The location is convenient.	1	2	3	4	5	1	2	3	4	5
19.	Forms are user friendly.	1	2	3	4	5	1	2	3	4	5
20.	The technology used is up-to-date.	1	2	3	4	5	1	2	3	4	5

Name _____ (optional) Phone number _____
Thanks for taking the time to help us serve you better! Please fold and return.

Exhibit 10.3 Customer satisfaction SERVQUAL survey.

else. Other common questions usually relate to common support functions, such as selling, communication, invoicing, order accuracy, and cycle time. Specific service or product features need to change for the particular market segment being surveyed.

Order selection and delivery:
(Check one)

	Excellent	Good	Fair	Poor	Terrible
1. How accurate is the selection of your order?	❏	❏	❏	❏	❏
2. How "on time" is the delivery?	❏	❏	❏	❏	❏
3. How do you rate the neatness of our drivers?	❏	❏	❏	❏	❏
4. What is the condition of the products at the time of delivery?	❏	❏	❏	❏	❏
5. What has been your experience with our product availability?	❏	❏	❏	❏	❏
6. What has been your experience with our bar codes?	❏	❏	❏	❏	❏

Comments:

Customer service and order
department: (Check one)

	Excellent	Good	Fair	Poor	Terrible
7. Overall, how do you rate our customer service department?	❏	❏	❏	❏	❏
8. How quickly are credit requests granted for shortages?	❏	❏	❏	❏	❏
9. How knowledgeable are our customer service people?	❏	❏	❏	❏	❏
10. When phoning our offices, how quickly is your call transferred?	❏	❏	❏	❏	❏
11. How responsive are we in returning your phone calls?	❏	❏	❏	❏	❏

Comments:

Sales department:
(Check one)

	Excellent	Good	Fair	Poor	Terrible
12. Overall, how do you rate the usefulness of our sales representatives' visits to your company?	❏	❏	❏	❏	❏
13. How do you rate his/her merchandising knowledge?	❏	❏	❏	❏	❏
14. How do you rate his/her product knowledge?	❏	❏	❏	❏	❏

Comments:

Exhibit 10.4   Distribution company satisfaction survey.

Pricing:
(Check one)

	Excellent	Good	Fair	Poor	Terrible
15. How do you rate our everyday wholesale prices?	❏	❏	❏	❏	❏
16. How attractive are our volume discount programs?	❏	❏	❏	❏	❏
17. How attractive are our volume purchase deals?	❏	❏	❏	❏	❏
18. Overall, how do you rate our monthly specials publication?	❏	❏	❏	❏	❏

Comments:

Consumer flyer program (looking good, feeling good):
(Check one)

	Excellent	Good	Fair	Poor	Terrible
19. Overall, how do you rate the format of our flyers?	❏	❏	❏	❏	❏
20. How do you rate the product selection?	❏	❏	❏	❏	❏
21. How do you rate the retail pricing on promoted products?	❏	❏	❏	❏	❏
22. What has been your experience with our in-stock performance on flyer items?	❏	❏	❏	❏	❏
23. Overall, how do you rate the quality of our window banners?	❏	❏	❏	❏	❏

Comments:

How would you rate our employees regarding courteousness and helpfulness?
(Check one)

	Excellent	Good	Fair	Poor	Terrible
24. Customer service representatives	❏	❏	❏	❏	❏
25. Sales representatives	❏	❏	❏	❏	❏
26. Order desk representatives	❏	❏	❏	❏	❏
27. Telephone receptionists	❏	❏	❏	❏	❏
28. Truck drivers	❏	❏	❏	❏	❏
29. Credit department	❏	❏	❏	❏	❏
30. Buyers	❏	❏	❏	❏	❏
31. Data processing	❏	❏	❏	❏	❏
32. Management	❏	❏	❏	❏	❏

Miscellaneous

	Excellent	Good	Fair	Poor	Terrible
33. How would you rate the range of products offered in our catalog?	❏	❏	❏	❏	❏
34. How convenient and easy to use is our catalog?	❏	❏	❏	❏	❏

Exhibit 10.4   (*Continued*).

How do we compare?

Example

Please write in the names of the three distributors you use most often. Evaluate each company's performance using this scale:

A = The best
B = Above average
C = Average, same as their competition
D = Needs improvement
F = Terrible
N = No opinion

Acme Distributors
Write in your primary distributor's name.

Pacific Wholesalers
Write in your secondary distributor's name.

On-Time Distribution Co.
Write in your third most often used distributor.

35.	Overall customer service	F
36.	Dependable, on-time delivery	C

Write in your primary distributor's name.

Write in your secondary distributor's name.

Write in your third most often used distributor.

35.	Overall customer service			
36.	Dependable, on-time delivery			
37.	Driver courtesy and skill			
38.	Salesperson knowledge			
39.	In-stock performance			
40.	Order selection accuracy			
41.	Resolves mistakes quickly			
42.	Responsive to special needs			
43.	Price			
44.	Promotional programs			
45.	Product selection			
46.	Credit terms and policies			
47.	Overall impression			

48. Have you taken advantage of any of our special services such as:

	Yes	No
Price stickers	❏	❏
Custom pricing	❏	❏
Guidelines reports	❏	❏
Consumer flyer program	❏	❏
Electronic ordering	❏	❏

Exhibit 10.4   Distribution company satisfaction survey.

Please rate the most important aspects of choosing a distribution company by allocating 100 points among the following categories:

Points
_____49. On-time delivery
_____50. Accurate order fulfillment
_____51. Problem solving
_____52. Price
_____53. Sales service
_____54. Undamaged goods

100 points total

What do you like best about our company?_____
_____
_____
_____

What do you like least about our company?_____
_____
_____
_____

Additional comments or suggestions: _____
_____
_____
_____

Your name _____
(optional)

Exhibit 10.4   Distribution company satisfaction survey.

Customer Value Maps

Definition

A customer value map compares price and quality to give customer-perceived value. Customers have a perception of the relative quality of products or services and their relative price. The value map shows how price and quality are related (see Exhibit 10.5). Within the fair value quadrant, customers perceive that they are getting their money's worth. In the upper left quadrant, customers believe that they were overcharged. In the lower right quadrant, customers perceive that they received more than their money's worth.

Benefits

As was mentioned before, AT&T found that only when it included price and competition in its measures were customer satisfaction scores related to market share predictions. The ability to predict whether customers will continue to buy your product or service is critical for strategic, quality, and financial planning. The value map makes this price/quality relationship easy to understand.

How?

Exhibit 10.5 shows the points at which price and features are related. Relative price scores are shown in Exhibit 10.6. As you can see, customers are asked to compare your prices with competitors' prices in the same class. A relative quality profile is shown in Exhibit 10.7.

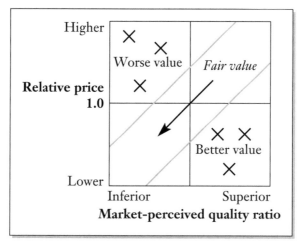

Exhibit 10.5   Customer value map.

Price satisfaction attributes	Importance weights	Acura	Other	Ratio
1	2	3	4	5 = 3/4
Purchase price	60	9	7	1.29
Insurance rates	20	6	6	1.00
Resale price	10	9	8	1.13
Finance rates	10	7	7	1.00
	100			
Price satisfaction score		8.3	7.0	
Price competitiveness score				1.18
Transaction price	Acura	Other	Ratio
a	b	c	d = b/c
Perceived	32.8	40	.82
Actual	35.2	40	.88

Exhibit 10.6   Market perceived price profile: luxury cars.

Reprinted with permission of the Free Press, a division of Simon & Schuster from *Managing Customer Value: Creating Quality and Service That Customers Can See* by Bradley T. Gale. Copyright © 1994 by Bradley T. Gale.

Quality attributes	Endo-surgery	Traditional surgery	Ratio	Relative weight	Weight X Ratio
At-home recovery	1–2 weeks	6–8 weeks	3.0	40	120
Hospital stay	1–2 days	3–7 days	2.0	30	60
Complications rate	0–5%	1–10%	1.5	10	15
Operation time	0.5–1 hour	1–2 hours	2.0	15	30
Postoperative scar	0.5–1 inch	3–5 inches	1.4	0.05	0.07
				100	
	Market-perceived quality score				232

Exhibit 10.7   Quality profile: Gallbladder operations, endo-surgery vs. traditional surgery.

Reprinted with permission of the Free Press, a division of Simon & Schuster from *Managing Customer Value: Creating Quality and Service That Customers Can See* by Bradley T. Gale. Copyright © 1994 by Bradley T. Gale.

Focus Groups and Interviews

Definition

Focus groups consist of six to 12 well-selected customers gathered for a specific purpose. Focused interviews are one-on-one telephone or face-to-face interviews with the same mission.

Sampling Process

Most focus interviewees or focus group participants are not randomly sampled. People are chosen because of the following factors.

- Their likelihood to participate
- Their value as a customer
- Their ability to articulate issues
- Convenience

Thus, the sample is not representative, and any conclusions need to be tested over a broad, stratified random sample.

A new type of convenience sampling is taking hold: Focus groups are emerging on the Internet. The Internet provides an easy way of sampling at a low cost. Be sure you qualify participants on their job titles, how frequently they use your product, purchase volume, and so on, so that you can track results. Also, you probably would be wise to do a sample reality check of some of the participants against your customer database to make sure you aren't getting responses from individuals not qualified to answer (kids or nonusers). Companies typically pay Internet focus group members about $30–$50 for each session.

Purposes of Focus Interviews or Groups

The purpose of a focus group can vary along the following lines. The word(s) in parentheses represents the best methodology according to my experience.

- *Invent the future.* Customers brainstorm about future services and products (groups—especially while using or after using the product/service; individual suggestions; ideas from the Internet).

- *Satisfaction.* Customers define the nuances of satisfiers and dissatisfiers (groups and individual).
- *Pricing.* Customers provide feedback on price vs. features (individual and Internet).
- *Ad-hoc problems.* Customers provide ideas on how to resolve special product or service issues (groups, individual, Internet).
- *Testing.* Customers test advertising, services, or products and give feedback (groups and/or individual, Internet).

Focus groups differ from advisory groups in that focus groups usually meet once and disband. Advisory groups meet over a defined period of time, and discussion items for advisory groups may be more open. Advisory group membership is usually staggered in one- to two-year rotations.

Benefits

Focus groups and interviews allow a trained facilitator to dig more deeply and define latent needs of customers. Likewise, the group dynamic sparks less conscious areas of customer needs as the participants bounce ideas off each other.

Sega of America, a $1 billion company in Redwood City, California, produces video games for teenagers. It produces new video games at a relentless pace—about 65 a year. It now outscores the once-dominant Nintendo in the U.S. video game market by knowing its customers. Edward Volkwein, senior vice president of marketing, says, "Kids' number one desire is to be up on new stuff all the time and know things that their parents don't know."

How can Sega be so sure? Sega conducts focus groups two or three times weekly. Staff members from Sega's ad agency, Goodby Berline & Silverstein, hang out with 150 kids in their bedrooms and go shopping with them.[2] Sega found that kids shop like adults, comparing prices and reading trade magazines. These contacts with kids are a combination of focused interviews, observation, and focus groups.

Focus groups are used to test advertising before it airs. The best bet is to not let the focus group design your creative ad (committee-designed ads can mangle any good copy), but let them tell you if you are inadvertently alienating them. Several focus groups I have conducted on advertising revealed that customers thought an ad was too sexist (advertising a woman's product from a male point of view). A paper products company killed a toilet tissue commercial when southern viewers perceived a sexual innuendo in the central image—a seven-year-old girl wearing a nightgown in bed. The ad agency had not perceived it.

How?

Conducting a focused interview with one person at a time versus conducting a focus group is frequently an issue. Some customers (at high levels) are very hard to reach. The focused interview may be the most practical for them.

Focused interviews are becoming increasingly popular as companies realize that focus groups have their own dynamics and can distort individual opinions because of group pressure. A study of 4000 companies conducted by the Management Roundtable and Product Development Consulting found that best-in-class companies interview individually so that interviewers could ask in-depth questions.[3] Focused interviews allow shy individuals to not be influenced by dominant group members. Sensitive issues (pricing, buying influences such as a boss) are particularly difficult for people to discuss in group settings.

Marketers historically have assumed that focus groups were more efficient and therefore cheaper than one-on-one interviews. Abbie Griffin of the University of Chicago did a study and found that as much information surfaced about complex office equipment in eight two-hour focus groups as in nine one-hour, one-on-one interviews.[4] Either is fine unless sensitive issues are present.

Invitations

How people are invited makes a big difference in whether they will participate. The invitation should include a statement about why that person was chosen: "We selected you because you are a target customer and can help us tailor our service or product to meet your needs." Exhibit 10.8 illustrates such an invitation.

If the customer's use of your product or service has little relationship to his or her personal or professional success, you may have to be

Dear Customer:

We would like to invite you to a Company X focus group that will be held Thursday, June 4, from 6:00 P.M.–8:30 P.M. A focus group is a group of about 10 select customers who can help us understand preferences on Product/Service X. We have selected you because you are one of our gold customers. As such, we recognize that you use our product/service extensively and that any improvements we make may benefit you. Thus, a deeper understanding of your needs and preferences is vital.

We are offering a catered dinner after the hour-and-a-half focus group. The dinner will offer you the opportunity to network with other local industry leaders. We will also hold a prize drawing for the 10 participants, with a first prize of $100 and second and third prizes of $50.

The logistics are as follows:

Time and date:	6:00 P.M.–8:30 P.M. on Thursday, June 4
Location:	Company name and address
RSVP by 6/1 to:	Jane Smith
	555-555-5555

We sincerely hope that you can participate in the meeting.

Exhibit 10.8   Sample focus group invitation.

more seductive in your invitation. Incentives should be increased if your customers have little motivation to help you improve your product. Paying people money helps, but offering a larger sum in a drawing seems to be even more of a motivation. Some cellular companies pay $35 for participation, and fast food restaurants pay up to $125 to achieve their desired sample. Serving food definitely helps.

Where and When to Hold the Focus Group

Several marketing firms have focus group facilities with one-way mirrors. These mirrors allow managers to observe real-time feedback, and usually the direct observation of customers' feelings makes suggestions easier to implement. Focus groups that encourage customers to test products are best done in facilities with videotape equipment. Too much happens when watching customers sample products or services; it is important to videotape the events so you don't miss anything.

One of the most important considerations in where you hold a focus group is convenience. The companies I work with that are involved in business-to-business selling usually look for a convenient way to organize focus groups before, during, or after conventions or professional meetings.

Meeting times need to be convenient for participants. Many retailers I have done focus groups with prefer morning times, because their traffic picks up after 11 A.M. Executives tend to prefer breakfasts or cocktail hour groups. Executives, not surprisingly, like it when groups are held at luxury resorts with golf and other sports available.

Tips

1. Use a neutral facilitator to conduct the focus group or interviews. If you use internal people, make sure they are thoroughly trained in how to be neutral. Salespeople or managers usually have a very difficult time learning how to be neutral.

2. Have a focus for your focus group. Do not try to accomplish too much in the one or two hours you have.

3. Start the focus group by expressing its purpose and telling why the participants were invited. Set the stage by emphasizing the importance of honest answers. Let participants know that there is room for diverse opinions; they do not have to come to consensus about any of the issues. Manage their expectations by telling them that you are soliciting input from multiple sources and will make decisions that fit the needs of the majority. You don't want to create an expectation that you will be acting on every suggestion.

4. Record the session with an audiotape or videotape. Let participants know you are taping the session and offer to stop the tape if they feel the need to. The tape recordings are helpful in communicating the strength of customer needs to management.

5. After the session, write thank-you notes to the participants and inform them of the changes that resulted from the focus group feedback.

Lost Customer Surveys

Definition

Lost customer surveys are interviews with customers who have stopped buying your product or service or significantly reduced their usage. Normally these surveys are done by phone so that the interviewer can probe areas of dissatisfaction.

Benefits

- Lost customer research has a high rate of return on investment. Lost customers can become extremely loyal if you fix their problem.

- Finding the reasons why customers defect helps you understand your competition.

How?

1. Define how *lost customer* is defined. Is a lost customer someone that has not bought your product in one month, two months, or a year?

2. Define who is responsible for identifying lost customers and by when.

3. Telephone surveys are most common for lost customer surveys.

4. The introduction is important. Lost customers have little motivation to help you since they usually have already gone through a "divorce" process. Tell them the interview will take only a few minutes and that their input is important for you to improve your service/product quality.

5. Introduce the purpose at the beginning of the interview, for example, "We noticed that you have not purchased (our product or service) in *x* (days, months, and so on) and would like to find out what influenced your decision not to renew."

6. Understand that the lost customer may throw out a smokescreen reason for nonpurchase at first, such as "I found your product/service too expensive." Probe. "Does that mean that you found something else that met your needs for a lower price?"

7. If the customer switched to a competitor's product, ask which features drew the customer to that product.

8. Make sure you understand the customer's purchase criteria and purchase process. You need to ask the customer if he or she was the sole decision maker if you have any doubt. You may need to speak to the real decision maker.

9. Ask the customer, "What would it take to win back your business?" This question holds the highest potential for uncovering problems that can recover a lost customer.

Who?

Lost customer surveys can either be done by a neutral outside company or by a neutral insider. They should not be conducted by the salesperson who was responsible for the customer. Sometimes the customer will not be as honest with a salesperson as with a neutral outsider. Likewise, the salesperson may not be honest about customers' responses if he or she is partially responsible for problems causing the customer to leave.

Tips

1. Interviewers making the calls should be empowered to make decisions while on the phone if they see that a customer can be saved. Spending limits should be defined ahead of time.

2. Exacting standards for feedback to appropriate people must be part of the system definition. The more time that elapses before a problem is resolved, the less chance there is of recovery. Feedback to appropriate decision makers should be immediate.

3. Lost customer data should be analyzed. Themes and decibel levels can be determined through cluster analysis and then developing check sheets from that analysis to tabulate comments. A Pareto chart can visually illustrate the main dissatisfiers. If the customers switched from your product to a competitor's product because of new features offered by the competition, those desirable features should be presented in a Pareto chart as well. These data get incorporated in the strategic quality planning process.

4. Track revenue recovered from the recovery of lost customers.

5. Look at the lost customer list and see if there are any patterns. Were lost customers all from small companies that ended up in finan-

cial trouble? Maybe the salespeople should focus on companies that are more financially solid. Did lost customers mostly leap to the competition? Serious benchmarking needs to happen. Are the larger accounts leaving? Perhaps partnership skills are lacking.

6. Compile some of your success stories that fully describe how customers were recovered. Normally, recovery takes a team effort. Publicize the names of people who contributed and what the lifetime value of the customer was.

Mystery Shoppers

Definition

Mystery shoppers pose as customers of the targeted company and test the service quality. They usually have a structured set of questions and experiences to evaluate as they shop. The stores or companies then take the feedback and determine what training or hiring processes need to change.

Benefits

In manufacturing, defects can be measured and controlled. In service, defects frequently happen in the form of a growl from an employee, an incorrect response, or long periods of waiting. A visit from upper management causes all kinds of red carpet behavior to roll out. Mystery shoppers can unobtrusively evaluate what typical customers experience.

How?

Mystery shoppers have to be just that—a mystery. Knowing that mystery shoppers are coming at a particular time changes behavior. Knowing who they will be takes the mystery out of this tool. Thus, companies usually contract their mystery shopping with an outside firm.

Who?

Outside firms normally do mystery shopping for companies. Sometimes out-of-town employees can do mystery shopping for a sister organization. They should not be able to be recognized, though.

Executives and employees should be encouraged and rewarded for being mystery shoppers with competitors' products or services. As part of the business advisory board for Delta, we encouraged upper management to fly Singapore Airlines to benchmark unmatched service. Singapore Airlines has 22 flight attendants per 747 rather than the typical 12. That makes a difference in the level of service the flight attendants can provide.

Tips

1. Look for ways to make it fun. Have mystery shoppers give some type of award or gift for service above and beyond the call of duty.

2. Allow employees to decide whether they want mystery shoppers. They will be much more receptive to feedback if they have invited this assessment tool.

3. Do mystery shopping at a variety of intervals over time. Doing it just once doesn't tell you much. You constantly have new employees and new services that need to be continuously tested.

4. Understand that mystery shopping is not a scientific measurement tool. The ability to observe small differences, check for enforcement of policies, and calibrate customer service are some of the values of mystery shopping. The Federal Aviation Authority has been doing mystery shopping for decades on the airlines. Their main concern is whether regulations are being enforced—seats upright on take-off and landing, baggage stowed, and so on.

New Customer Feedback

Definition

New customer feedback is a specially designed survey initiated shortly after the customer has sampled the service or product. The University of Colorado at Boulder conducts new student surveys to find out about the registration and orientation process. New customer feedback surveys measure the ease of customer entry into the company.

Benefits

First impressions of a service or product are vital. I bought the most expensive model fax machine I could find in hopes that it would do everything I wanted. The manual was so complicated that I took the

fax machine back even though I am an electronics junkie. I will probably never buy that brand again. The problem was partially caused by
the lack of clear directions, and partly caused by the crystal-clear
instructions on my previous Panasonic model. I knew I had a choice,
and didn't want to waste time. Some of the high-tech companies we
work with have return rates as high as 30 percent.

In addition to capturing potential lost customers, a new customer
survey can personalize your product or service. Several medical and
dental clinics in southern California have initiated this practice of calling customers after the first visit to ask how they are feeling and how
the clinic's services rated. Hearing from a provider makes us feel that
we are special. Now if they can just shorten the waiting time before
appointments!

How?

Some of the popular questions to ask new customers are the following:

1. How did you hear about us?
2. What were the most important features in making this purchase decision?
3. What other products or services did you consider?
4. What did you like better about our product or service?
5. How did we rate (1 = low, 5 = high) for our service/product
   introduction (manuals, instructions, and so on).
6. What was your level of satisfaction with our packaging, manuals, and installation?
7. What was your level of satisfaction with the waiting time for
   the product/service?

The survey can ask for numbers in a Likert scale and then probe for
improvements in open-ended questions.

Another feature that can be added is a new customer orientation.
Charles Schwab does this orientation with new customers to help customers use its services more efficiently. The orientation also helps
develop a personal touch in what is primarily a telephone service. New
customer orientations can be enormously helpful in averting confusion in using the product or service.

Observation

Definition

Observation can be done both by employees or on videotape. Marriott trains employees to observe nonverbal signals of customers and proactively respond to building frustration. Ritz Carlton encourages employees to not only observe customer behavior but also record it so that system issues can be identified.

Benefits

Observation is a powerful tool to assess how customers react to or use your product. You can also see how they respond to your competitors' service or product by watching the customers in action. Going for the gold means doing everything right; the only way you have to assess this level of detail is to watch customers actually using your product or service. A written survey or a focus group is too far removed from all of the reminders of the details that matter to high-usage customers.

Observation provides the main opportunity for both real-time measurement and a "real-time" fix. Customer satisfaction research shows a strong relationship between fixing problems immediately and retaining customers. Thus, this seemingly simple tool can have a major impact on the bottom line.

A second level of observation is using video recorders to reveal areas of customer dissatisfaction. The following examples illustrate some uses.

- Honda videotapes automobile drivers to see how they use the equipment in cars.
- Spa Resort Hawaiian (Deming Prize winner in Japan) uses video recorders to define appropriate waiting times for check-in lines at the hotel. People start fidgeting when they are impatient. Staffing levels are then defined by that observed ideal waiting time.
- Spa Resort Hawaiian uses video recorders to assess the appropriate temperature of the ambient air in its covered mineral spa area. If people are too cold, they quickly pick up their towels and dry off.

Marketing giants like Procter & Gamble videotape customers sampling their products to see how they react.

Tips

Observation requires skill-based training for employees. Training usually involves having employees look for particular things.

- Waiting times—when customers show signs of restlessness
- How customers use the product or service (ease of use, when they slow down, what questions new users ask, and so on)
- Satisfiers and dissatisfiers as they move through the experience
- Flow of customers across several functions (at banks, first class vs. coach check-in times at airlines, customs checkpoints, and so on)

Decisions about observational data can be used to test temperatures of swimming pools, staffing levels needed at different times of the day, or new features that make the product or service easier to use. Examples of such features are as follows:

- Lower-level shelf on a check-in counter—to set down a briefcase or purse down while checking in (many Delta Crown Room lounges in airports)
- Longer straps on purses (optional) that enable women to put a purse over the shoulder to free up hands
- Cup holders for trucks or cars (most have done this)
- Positioning of instruments on the dashboard
- Spaces needed by pilots in the cockpit for their chart briefcase
- Red coats or line watchers at the check-in counter at the airport to redirect customers who are needlessly waiting because they already have a ticket

Many of the pilots and flight attendants with whom I have spoken over millions of air miles have mentioned the ease of use of the Boeing 757 and the Boeing 777. Boeing engineers watched the way pilots and attendants went about their duties on actual flights. The engineers observed personnel using dry ice instead of a refrigerator, the difficult height and slope of baggage compartments, and so on. They watched pilots' eyes travel back and forth across the instruments to determine where to place those instruments. They watched the pilots struggle with locating a place to put their charts. Then they talked to pilots and flight attendants to solicit other ideas. As I listen to the pilots and flight attendants talk about their airplane preferences, they have rave reviews for Boeing. That is in contrast to complaints I have heard about how some airplanes fly nose high at cruise speed. That forces the flight attendants to constantly move the heavy beverage and food cart uphill.

Observation also requires that you train employees in how to track problem areas. If half of the bellhops observe that people wander around the pool when they are looking for the restaurant, it may be a good idea to put up better signs. At a computer superstore, I asked what the difference was between a DX model and an SX model of a certain computer. It took several minutes to track down a salesperson to ask the question. He laughed and replied, "Oh, everybody asks that question! I must have 20 people a day ask." My next question was, "Why don't you put up a sign?" It would save customers lots of frustration and wasted time.

Regular meetings or incentives should be developed to pull the observations together and develop action items to prevent frequent problems. This harks back to rewards for employee suggestions.

A company culture of "fixing problems" is important.

Perceptual Research

Definition

Perceptual research measures how a total customer pool perceives your company compared to the competition. That customer pool includes your customers, your competitors' customers, and any potential customers.

Benefits

Using only those names from your own customer database gives you a *very* distorted picture of the real world. Your customer database works for your customer satisfaction measures; it doesn't for perceptual research. A whole group of people with special needs may buy from your competitors. Some of them are fiercely loyal. Why? The best pool of new customers for you comes from your competitors. Your competitors are probably offering features you may not even know about. Thus, perceptual research helps you determine your perceived market value. The results are false if you are not going the distance to retrieve names of competitors' decision makers. That does not mean just using your customers who also do business with your competitors.

How?

The best way to do perceptual research is with a blind study. That means that customers do not know the sponsoring organization(s), so they don't distort their answers to please that particular organization. Many companies find that they need to hire an outside company. Customers will sometimes ask who is sponsoring the study, and an insider would have to lie about which company he or she works for.

If you use an outside firm and are doing business-to-business selling, make sure you hire a research company that specializes in dealing with more technical and/or business-to-business customers. You will need that sophistication to get through to decision makers. You will also need to train the research people on your specific products or services.

Having the research company invite your competitors to do jointly sponsored research is the ideal method for perceptual research. It decreases the costs and increases the accuracy of contact names. Only a few companies do business-to-business research well. Many market or customer research firms know consumer research. They offer excellent services with scanning devices and sound statistical sampling. They can do consumer research very efficiently. But with business-to-business research, you need researchers who know how to ask quantitative questions and then probe. In the past we tried to subcontract with many of these well-known consumer research companies to help our larger business-to-business clients, with disastrous results. The short-term price was right; the long-term price included trying to heal the irritations expressed by perceptual survey recipients when they tried to add comments. Customers became highly irritated if the researcher didn't have a clue about the business, the products, or anything outside of the highly structured questions.

J.D. Powers has been doing research sponsored for automobile competitors for years. Competitive Edge, in Fountain Valley, California, has also been doing business-to-business research, higher-end customer research, and technical research. The results are usually given such that you see your rank in the various categories but don't see your competitors' names attached to the other rankings. This preserves the privacy and dignity of the system.

Typical Questions

1. From whom have you purchased product/service X?
   a_____ b_____ c_____

2. Who do you believe is the best supplier of X? _____

3. Why do you rank them as first?

4. What features do you consider important when you buy X? Please list the features in the first column below. In the second column, fill in which features are more important to you by spreading 100 points among the features. Spend the most points on those features that are most important to you; the total points should add up to 100. In the third column, please indicate the company or product that best provides that feature.

Feature	Points	Company that best provides the feature
_____	_____	_____
_____	_____	_____
_____	_____	_____
_____	_____	_____
_____	_____	_____

100 total points

5. Check which best applies and fill in the appropriate blank.

   The next time I buy (product or service X):

   ____a. I will check with _____ (which provider of product/service X) first.

   ____b. I will think of buying only from _____ .

   ____c. I do not know.

Mixing Perceptual with Satisfaction Research

Many companies try to combine customer satisfaction and perceptual information. That works only when you have customers who buy from you and from your competitors and are not linked to either of you. Mixing both does not allow you to do a blind survey, which is much more accurate than one identifying you as the originator.

Tips

1. Include an incentive to complete the survey. Random drawings with a cash reward work very well.

2. Expect the response rate to be lower than for your customer satisfaction survey. You need to aim for at least an 80 percent response rate in your target customer satisfaction survey. In perceptual research, 30 percent to 40 percent is more realistic. The reason is that customers perceive a customer satisfaction survey as a personal way to be included in your decision making. Perceptual research doesn't have the personal payoff because the originator is not known and many telemarketing firms have created mistrust about customer or marketing surveys. Telemarketers sometimes start with a survey and end with a sales pitch.

3. CATI (computer-aided telephone interviewing) systems can help you collate the data. One of the least expensive and easiest to customize is Survey Pro ($795).

Real-Time Fixes

Definition

Real-time fixes happen as an interviewer is talking to a customer. The customer either calls to complain or is contacted in a proactive customer satisfaction survey. Real-time fixes also happen when an employee observes that a customer is dissatisfied and offers to help. In reality, this is not a separate tool but is an advanced stage embedded in complaint tracking, customer satisfaction surveys, and observation. The interviewer has the authority to fix the problem or provide a refund to compensate for the company's error.

Benefits

Dissatisfied customers' problems can frequently be fixed. The dissatisfied customers will actually be more loyal if their problems are fixed immediately than if the problems go unsolved.

> *Real-time fixes are probably the most powerful tool for driving revenues in this entire tool collection.*

A TARP survey of high-tech equipment buyers found that 63 percent of all dissatisfied customers will never do business with an offending company again. If a supplier resolves its problems, 90 percent of those dissatisfied customers remain loyal to the supplier. Emphasis on real-time fixes can show up on the bottom line immediately.[5]

How?

Often customers just want an apology. GTE Directories sales and marketing manager, Marilyn Carlson, talked about how all of the salespeople and customer service representatives are empowered to rebate customers for problems. Ritz Carlton has a $2000 level of empowerment per employee to fix customer satisfaction issues as they happen. Marriott spent $700,000 training all of its employees on empowerment so that they could fix customer problems on-the-spot.[6]

Permission to make decisions isn't all that is needed. Training is needed to help employees understand how to handle problems and resolve issues. Training on the following topics is helpful.

- How to handle irate customers
- How to defuse anger
- How to problem solve and find solutions
- How to guide people through the action steps
- How to prevent customer abuse of the system
- Where to go for information and answers
- How to make the resolution or compensation for customers' problems commensurate with the size of the problem

The sixth topic is one of the most difficult in large organizations. Receptionists, salespeople, and anyone likely to have customer contact needs to be fully informed of the likely questions that will arise and where to find the answers. This requires a systematic look at what those typical customer questions are, what the common customer suggestions are, and what computer systems would help make information and answers more accessible for both employees and customers. Prepackaged answers can help the respondent provide facts.

Tracking systems need to ensure that these real-time fixes are closed out. The tracking systems typically parallel the customer complaint systems, since these two tools are closely related.

Who?

The hardest part of making real-time fixes happen is empowering employees. Trusting employees with spending limits can be difficult for managers from the "old school." Thus, all levels need to be involved to make this work. Employees also need extensive training in how to gauge appropriate fixes for customer dissatisfiers. I had a Marriott employee give me a free night because I waited for 10 minutes at the check-in counter. That was very generous, but unnecessary. You don't want employees to give away the shop when they are trying to make customers happy. Training them on how to calibrate dissatisfaction and how to ask the customer "What will it take to make you happy?" are vital in this process. Training managers not to berate employees for testing those limits is also part of preserving group enthusiasm.

The executive-level managers need to constantly remind employees that they have permission to truly satisfy customers. JC Penney's philosophy is that the lifetime worth of a customer is thousands of dollars. To drive a customer away by not refunding $30 for a defective pair of jeans does not serve JC Penney's long-term goals well.

Considerable training needs to be done with frontline employees to help them be truly empowered to fix problems. They need accurate information, access to customer records, a spending limit, and a freedom from fear for overstepping the bounds. Even the best companies can have difficulty with this. I have asked many employees in high-performing companies how many times they took advantage of their spending authority to fix problems. The response in many cases was "Never." When I probed, it was evident that these employees didn't trust their managers to support their decisions. The training needs to be backed up by hero stories that reinforce this satisfied customer theme from the management level. Likewise, employees need to understand that the fix need not be excessive in value. Waiving four months of health club dues for having to wait 10 minutes extra to check in isn't appropriate.

Tips

1. Train employees by role-playing real-life situations. Only then will they understand how to fix customer problems without giving away too much.

2. Help employees understand difficult personalities in the training.

3. Reward and recognize employees for resolving customer problems. Otherwise, they will hesitate to report the problem because they fear that it will be held against them. Without that tracking you have no idea whether the problem is an isolated case or a predominant customer dissatisfier.

Transaction Reports

Definition

Transaction reports are feedback pieces on transactions. Companies usually perform many types of transactions with customers. A hospital has registration, treatment, nursing services, food services, and billing. A bank has an automated teller service, live tellers, financial advisors, and monthly statements. A distribution company has order fulfillment, delivery cycle times, unloading, and problem solving. Each of these moments-of-truth customer contacts have the potential to either satisfy or irritate customers—usually not because of a single event, but a series of chronic irritations. Transaction reports measure the customer's reaction immediately following the transaction.

Real-time fixes are usually in response to observed or stated complaints; transaction reports solicit feedback from individuals who normally may not have expressed their reactions. Transaction surveys allow the surveyor to immediately fix the problem, if possible: real-time, every time customer satisfaction and measurement.

Benefits

Because transaction reports are proactive, they can uncover both satisfied and dissatisfied customers. Turning an unhappy customer into a happy one close to the point of the problem makes for loyal customers.

How?

1. Determine which transactions are worth monitoring.
2. Determine what percentage of those transactions you need to measure.
3. Decide how you will randomly sample those transactions.
4. Let customers know you will be monitoring these transactions periodically.
5. Condition their expectations by saying something like, "The quality of service to our valued customers is very important to us. We would appreciate hearing your reaction to the transaction you just completed."
6. Formulate simple questions. Typical questions are open ended.

Transaction Report Questions

- *What did you like about this transaction (invoice, fitting, meeting, report, and so on)?*

- *What suggestions do you have?*

- *On a scale of 1 to 5 (1 = low and 5 = high), what was your level of satisfaction?*

---

7. Transaction reports are brief. They are meant to seek ideas to improve the quality of the transaction, not to measure trends.
8. The value of transaction reports is particularly great for special events or projects. After each, debriefings of key participants should assess what went well and what needs improvement.

Who?

Each transaction (airline reservation, hotel check-in, ATM machine use, invoice, help-line call, and so on) is a possible candidate for a transaction report. Usually a systematic and scientific process is developed by the CSS steering committee, with samples at regular intervals.

Collecting and recording the data requires training and a positive incentive for turning in the reports. Management review, coaching, and recognition helps to make the change process easy.

Usability Tests

Definition

Usability tests reveal how people use the product. When a washing machine manufacturer in Japan did usability tests on its washing machines in the 1960s, it found that some customers were using them to wash potatoes.[7] In working with an integrated factory automation Windows-based software company, I found from customer service people that they are constantly amazed at the variety of purposes for which customers are using their software. One of the most frequent thoughts is, "But it wasn't designed for . . . ." That's the point! Learning how customers use your products enables you to have a competitive edge over the competition in designing it for how customers really use it.

Software companies usually conduct usability labs in their beta tests. Beta tests are early releases of the software to check compatibility issues with other software. The tester is supposed to give feedback to the software developer. When Microsoft did a beta test of Windows 4.0 in 1995, it sent 48,000 copies to industry testers. That was after it had done an internal test with 1000 employees to get the bugs out.[8] Contrast this 48,000 figure to the 350 beta testers that were used for Windows 3.0. Not only are customers demanding compatibility, but the increasing complexity of multimedia makes compatibility harder to achieve.

Bridgestone tires (Japanese owned) conducted usability tests by outfitting logging trucks with its tires. Bridgestone set up camp at the base of a mountain and analyzed each tire that came back with a problem. This was in contrast to Goodyear, which did most of its testing in the lab. You have to look at how people use your service or product in order to figure out what improvements are necessary.

At Mira Costa College in Oceanside, California, we designed a usability test that required management to register for classes as if they were students. We called this a *living flowchart*. This exercise made it harder for management to deny the problems that employees and students had been pointing out for years.

British Airways is one of the few airlines in Europe that has been profitable in recent years. I flew to London recently and a British

Airways researcher approached me after I had just gone through the line and customs check-in. Her questions were very focused on the "use of the check-in counter and the customs clearance." The questions also related to testing a new approach to the waiting line ("Would you rather have one line for everybody, or several lines?"). The importance of the research is illustrated by a subtle nuance. The appearance of one line may seem fairer to those behind a desk making a decision. However, those of us who have to move luggage as we move up in the line see one line as a major inconvenience. You can't hear those preferences unless you catch people in the act of using your product.

In the research I did on first-class customers for Delta, I was constantly aware of how many more details of its service were apparent as passengers used the airline. Once the passenger stepped into the terminal, those nuances vanished into thin air. Interviews are best done as people *are experiencing* your product or service. Those details are what will make or break long-term customer retention.

Motorola noticed a radical increase in its pager revenues in Korea. When investigating how people there were using them, Motorola found that young women sometimes carried as many as seven pagers tucked into their waistband. Each pager represented a different boyfriend who was paging the woman—an exclusive communication link. The numbers of pagers a young woman wore was a status symbol.[9]

Usability studies help you segment your customer base. If you make microchips, you will find that the cellular phone industry's needs are very different than the chip requirements for defense satellite systems. Technical specifications are a given. What about the nuances of service specifications? Those service needs include co-development of design, knowledge of customer service workers, payment flexibility, depth of sales input, customized invoicing, and management presence with the customer.

With an airline, all elements of the service need to be designed appropriately for varying uses (leisure, business, and international), such as configuration of the airplane, meals, check-in service, customers, personalities of flight attendees, pricing, cleaning of lavatories, and extras available on flight (toys vs. airphones). A price-conscious family will put up with longer lines, less service, and smaller amounts of space. The flight attendants, however, need to learn to better deal with children. Business travelers want speed—to get through check in, board, and arrive at their destination quickly. Food preferences tend to be more health oriented, since airplane food is the staple diet of frequent flyers. Many of the airlines have tried to deal with this multiple-use issue by calibrating services according to sections of the airplane (business and coach). One international carrier found that the cleanliness of the bathrooms was the highest priority item for its international travelers.

Win/Loss Reports

Definition

Win/loss reports usually investigate the reasons why you won or lost a competitive bid. Engineering, communications, and government procurements frequently build in these debriefing sessions. The best forum is a face-to-face interview or a telephone call. Clients can get very uncomfortable putting reasons for not selecting you in writing.

Benefits

The win/loss interview can help you assess your strengths and weaknesses relative to the competition. The point of purchase is the most powerful moment of truth in finding out why people really buy your product or service. Organizations and individuals can list what is important to them in a survey and then make a completely different decision at the point of purchase.

How?

Questions should be gathered from those involved in the bid and incorporated into the set of interview questions. Not all of them will get addressed if the interview is shorter than you would like.

Many clients do not like to go through these interviews with companies that did not win the project. You may need to explain that you are "in this for the long term," and the feedback is vital to position your company to be more attractive in the next round. You might also plead the case that considerable resources were put into the bidding process, and the debriefing will help keep you from making the same mistakes again.

Start with open-ended questions such as the following:

- What was most important to you in this purchase decision?
- What special features did Company X provide over the competition?

- Please rank your priorities in what you wanted, from most important to least.

Then probe. This example is from a project-oriented engineering company.
How did we do relative to the competition on the following areas?

- Project manager we proposed
- Understanding of your requirements
- Understanding of the scope of work
- Unit rates (or other pricing patterns)
- Proposed project plan
- Teamwork
- Creative solutions for your problems
- Qualifications of proposed project personnel

You can ask the customer to rank order the competitors and then explain, or just leave the questions open ended.

Who?

A neutral party is the best interviewer for a win/loss report. If a member of the proposed team or a salesperson is involved in the interview, he or she must be coached not to explain or defend any issues. Honesty is very fragile in these interviews.

Tips

1. Do the interviews immediately after the win or loss. The trail gets cold quickly.
2. Don't forget to do a win debrief as well as a loss debrief. Winning can cover up a multitude of rocks beneath the surface of the water that you need to know about to navigate your way through other narrow passages.
3. Share the reports with the entire team. Negative feedback about individuals should be culled from the report and given individually.
4. Develop a corrective action plan right away before the energy dissipates.

5. An overall analysis of what recurrent themes are responsible
for both wins and losses should be conducted at least quarterly.

Notes

1. John J. Newbold, director of market research at Compaq, "Is It Compaq? Tracking Customer Satisfaction for the World's Largest PC Manufacturer" (speech given at the 8th Annual Customer Satisfaction and Quality Measurement Conference, Washington, D.C., 19 February 1996.)

2. Patricia Sellers, "20 Companies on a Roll," *FORTUNE*, autumn/winter 1993, 29.

3. Jon Brecka, "The Voice of the Customer Is Loud and Clear," *Quality Progress* 28, no. 5 (May 1995): 4.

4. Terence Pare, "How to Find Out What They Want," *FORTUNE*, autumn/winter 1993, 41.

5. Pamela Gordon, "Customer Satisfaction Research Reaps Rewards," *Quality* 32 (May 1993): 39–41.

6. Larry Armstrong and William Symonds, "Beyond May I Help You," *Business Week*, 25 October 1991, 100–102.

7. Noriaki Kano, interview by author, Tokyo, Japan, 1 October 1992.

8. Brad Stratton, "Talk to 48,000 Customers Lately?" *Quality Progress* 28, no. 4 (April 1995): 5.

9. Bill Okonski, logistics manager at Information Systems Group, interview by author, Dallas, Texas, 8 May 1996.

Chapter 11

Tools for Designing, Analyzing, and Synthesizing Data

Control Charts

Definition

A control chart is a managerial tool used to monitor a process to see whether that process is in statistical control. A certain amount of variation is normal in manufacturing and service processes. Sometimes phones get answered in one ring; sometimes in six. Sometimes a rod comes off a manufacturing line at 4.00002 feet, and sometimes at 3.998 feet. The upper control limit (UCL) and lower control limit (LCL) indicate how much variation is typical for the process. More than 99.97% of the results (three standard deviations or 3σ) fall within this UCL and LCL. Points that fall outside those limits indicate special cause rather than common cause variation. The control chart in Exhibit 11.1 plots quarterly overall customer satisfaction scores. As you can see, the normal variation of scores ranges from 92 percent to 96 percent over two years' time.

Benefits

One of the most difficult struggles when initiating a CSS is resisting the temptation to overreact to data. Perhaps the company is taking quarterly satisfaction measures and finds that in the third quarter the numbers go down. Those numbers may represent common cause, or normal, variation. That means that, given this division and its system, the numbers are likely to vary across time. Overmanaging is frequently worse than undermanaging. A control chart establishes the limits of normal variation so that management doesn't overreact when numbers go up or down slightly.

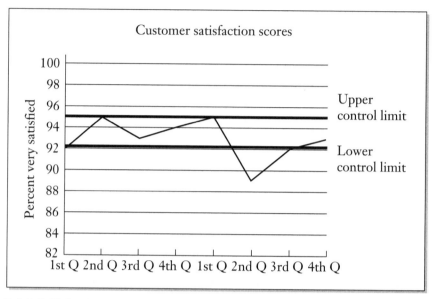

Exhibit 11.1   Control chart.

How to Use Control Charts

Control charts are one of the most popular tools used in both manufacturing and service firms. The concept behind the chart is critical to total quality manufacturing and total quality service. Control charts help identify what the current practices and systems can predictably yield. A bank may find that satisfaction scores vary over time from 92 percent very satisfied to 96 percent very satisfied. Over time, more than 99 percent of the facilities reveal that satisfaction level. A control chart would show that more than 99 percent of the error rates fall between 92 percent and 96 percent satisfied.

If managers react to each swing, they will find that the system can get worse. If managers don't like the range, they need to change the system. Hiring and training practices may need to change. The computer system may need to change. Micromanagers that react to every slight variation further disrupt a stable system. Managers need to work on the special causes of variation and change the systems so that they yield precise and predictable results.

Control charts are useful in a gold CSS when you are measuring large numbers, as in consumer research. One-on-one account value management is more appropriate for key accounts. Hopefully, your services or products are mass customized so that you can track satisfaction, value, competition, revenues, and profits one customer at a time for your key customers.

Graphs

Definition

Graphs are visual representations of data. The various types of graphs include bar charts, line charts, pie charts, area charts or scatter diagrams, or combinations of these (see Exhibit 11.2). Many graphs can be drawn with a three-dimensional effect.

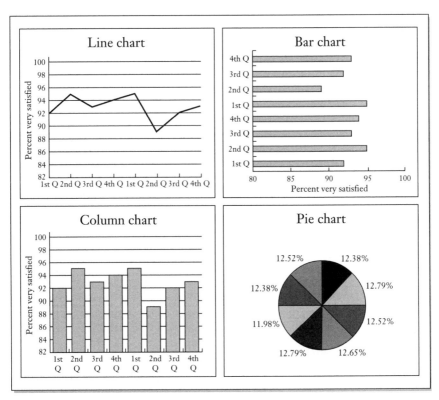

Exhibit 11.2   Types of graphs.

Benefits

Charts make data analysis and decision making easier for most people. A few rare individuals prefer to look at raw data, but they are the exception.

Pareto Charts

Definition

The Pareto Principle is named after a nineteenth-century economist, Vilfredo Pareto, who noticed an uneven distribution of wealth—20 percent of the people owned 80 percent of the wealth. Juran found that this uneven distribution was true in other areas as well—most trouble or opportunity comes from just a few causes. The Pareto chart helps to visually separate the "vital few" from the "trivial many" (see Exhibit 11.3).

Benefits

In this information age, managing data and making data useful for decisions are key. Focus is vital. Pareto charts make decision-making easier by organizing the data.

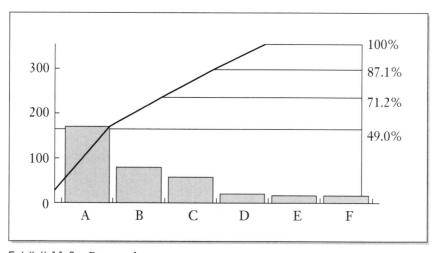

Exhibit 11.3   Pareto chart.

How to Use Pareto Charts

Pareto charts are helpful to display qualitative information. Complaints and suggestions frequently come from focus groups, complaint systems, and open-ended questions. Those who analyze the customer satisfaction data need to look for themes and decibel levels.

Themes are the items that are mentioned frequently in open-ended forums. Delivery times or inaccuracies on order forms may be recurrent issues raised by customers. Going through the complaints and focus group records and counting the frequency of mentions is helpful. Then making a Pareto chart of how frequently items are mentioned helps call attention to the vital few. The themes can be collected on one Pareto chart or charted separately for complaints, focus groups, user groups, observation, and other qualitative measures of customer satisfaction.

Reliability and Validity

Definition

Reliability relates to repeatability. It asks the question, "If you administered this same survey again, would you get the same results?" Interviewing someone right after a root canal procedure is likely to give a different result than after the person was just told about a promotion.

Validity relates to the question, "Is this instrument measuring what we want it to measure?" A customer satisfaction survey hopefully measures not only how satisfied customers are with your product or service, but how that preference relates to buying behavior. AT&T CCS, for instance, found it had highly satisfied customers but its market share was decreasing. It wasn't until it asked customers what was important to track (price was one item missed) that the measures started moving together.

Benefits

High-performing companies have precise instruments on their instrument panel. The instruments are carefully calibrated to make sure that little error is allowed. Decisions need to be made too quickly in highly competitive times to rely on faulty instruments.

How?

One of the main ways reliability is tapped is by asking similar questions many times in the same survey and then comparing those answers. Likewise, companies also test to see when a measurement produces the most reliable results. Gannett, for instance, found that data were more reliable if the survey was sent two weeks after, rather than two days after, it returned a serviced engine.

Qualitative tools like focus groups and open-ended questions take some special testing to make sure that themes or clusters have the same meaning to different people. You don't want your customer service group members all interpreting category titles in different ways on their check sheets.

Use interjudge reliability and operational definitions to help build reliability into the complaint check sheets (see Exhibit 11.4). Have

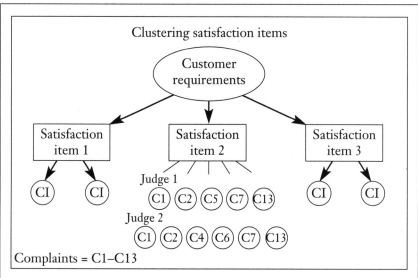

Use interjudge agreement to see if two or more judges agree that items fit in the same category, for example,

- Judge 1 puts items 1, 2, 5, 7, 9, and 13 into satisfaction item 2.
- Judge 2 puts items 1, 2, 4, 6, 7, 9, and 13 into satisfaction item 2.
- The interjudge agreement is 5/7, or 0.86.
- The recommended interjudge agreement is 0.8.
- If you have less than 0.8, have the judges talk to each other.

Exhibit 11.4   Interjudge reliability.

"judges" go through the themes, complaints, or suggestions and group them into common headings. Test the way in which several judges have clustered the customers' comments and then conduct an inter-judge reliability measure. If the measure is more than 80 percent, you have clusters that will be easily interpreted.

Revenue, Profit, and CSS Analysis

Definition

Revenue and profit analysis are much more common to most companies than the other elements in this book. What is relatively new is for executives to take an *integrated* look at the revenue, profit, quality, and customer satisfaction picture and focus on high-profit and high-growth areas. Market share is important, as is incremental margin (new money that goes directly to the bottom line because all the bills are paid).

Benefits

Performing simultaneous revenue, quality, customer satisfaction, and profit analyses allows you to focus on success. What will make your target clients most satisfied? What will make you most successful?

How?

The pie chart in Exhibit 11.5 provides a visual picture of the segments of a software company's contributions to overall profit. Which segment deserves the most attention? When this company analyzed how it spent time and resources, it discovered that the greatest amount of time was spent with university professors. Universities was such a small market segment that it didn't even appear on the pie chart! Yet professors received the product at the cheapest price, required the most assistance, and were the most demanding of services. The company decided to evaluate its pricing and customer service strategy to be more in line.

When?

The integrated look at revenue, profit, quality, and customer satisfaction is best done at the strategic quality planning retreat.

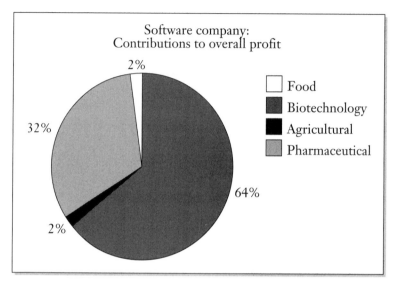

Exhibit 11.5   Pie chart.

Sampling and Sample Size

Definition

Companies frequently cannot afford to survey each and every customer. Consumer products are typical of this. AT&T cannot afford to sample 100 percent of its 80 million long-distance customers. If a company wants to optimize the money it spends on customer research, it must be scientific about the way it selects a sample of its customer base (sampling) and the number of customers it selects to represent the whole (sample size). Otherwise, strategic quality decisions may be made that are based on a biased sample of the customer base. If the squeaky wheels don't represent the whole, you can end up with a less satisfied group of customers than if you never measured.

Business-to-business organizations frequently have more of a problem with segmentation than with sampling. If you have only 300 key customers, why not sample everybody? The mere act of calling a customer in the CSS enhances the relationship (if done well). The purpose of the CSS is to measure, manage, and reengineer customer expectations and service as simultaneously as possible.

Benefits

Sampling allows CSSs to be more efficient and less costly. Larger samples require more time. Faster, better, and cheaper is the byline. Taking too long to conduct a survey can get you in trouble on the timeliness dimension. Still, the sample size must be representative enough and large enough to produce valid conclusions.

How?

Desirable sample size is based on two statistically based decisions.

1. What margin of error do you want?
2. What level of confidence do you desire?

For instance, if your company will be making large equipment decisions before going ahead with a product launch, you want the margin of error to be low (plus or minus 1 percent). You would also want the confidence in the results to be high. This means that your statistically determined confidence level needs to be plus or minus 5 percent or less. On the other hand, perhaps you won't be using the data to make high-cost or high-stakes decisions. Settling for a 5 percent margin of error and 10 percent level of confidence means substantially fewer numbers of people need to be sampled. Determining these two measures should be assisted by a qualified statistician.

A second key element in accurate and unbiased response is the sampling process. Most companies I work with use a stratified random sampling process. The companies segment their customers into industry segments, geographical segments, or loyalty segments, then randomly sample within each segment.

Randomly sampling customers is not as easy as it sounds. One-half of the households in some metropolitan areas now have unlisted telephone numbers.[1] In Las Vegas, 57 percent of phone numbers are unlisted. Unlisted phone numbers are also common in California. Likewise, even telephone surveys that randomly sample unlisted numbers that are randomly generated end up with many missed calls. Also, who's to say that people who are active and not at home to answer a call are the same population as those who stay at home?

Who?

Determining sample sizes, sampling methods, and segmentation are areas where outside help is warranted if the company does not have experts inside. Too many specific variables can influence those decisions.

Scatter Diagrams

Definition

A scatter diagram is a simple way to relate two attributes. You might want to use a scatter diagram to find out whether there is a correlation between how many times someone has used your product and satisfaction level. You might want to determine the relationship between the time spent waiting in line and overall satisfaction. A scatter diagram allows you to plot these two attributes and see if they move up or down together. The closer the dots approximate a straight line, the higher their correlation. Factor analysis is another statistical process used to relate one item to another.

Benefits

Scatter diagrams are an easy visual way to see a possible relationship between two variables. Sometimes they make it easier for managers to make decisions than a straight correlation coefficient. Note that the dots tend to move together in Exhibit 11.6. If the waiting time and level of satisfaction were not related, the dots would be all over the chart.

How?

See the example scatter diagram in Exhibit 11.6.

Who?

Managers can draw simple scatter diagrams rather than having to rely on statisticians to do correlation coefficients. Keep in mind that relationships do not show that one variable necessarily causes another.

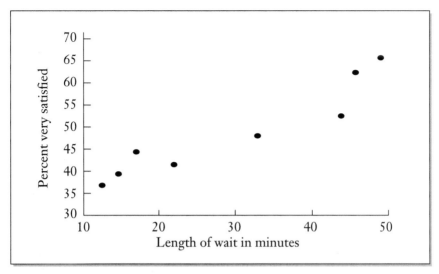

Exhibit 11.6   Scatter diagram.

Note

1. Alan Dutka, *AMA Handbook for Customer Satisfaction: A Complete Guide to Research Planning and Implementation* (Lincolnwood, Ill.: NTC Business Books, 1994), 67.

Chapter 12

Tools for Using the Data

Celebrations

Definition

Celebrations capture the positive spirit with tangible items that are integral to a customer satisfaction system, such as certificates of appreciation, high fives in the hall, award luncheons, or any other creative way of recognizing progress or a job well done. Employees who do the volume of work needed to gather and analyze data and then turn it into positive results for customers need constant reinforcement. Money and time need to be budgeted for this frequently ignored area.

Benefits

Customer satisfaction is best managed by the pull theory rather than the push theory. Having positive recognition systems in place with tangible symbols of success for results does more to enhance productivity than reprimands for not meeting goals.

A survey illustrated the importance of this dimension. Management Decision Systems in Darien, Connecticut surveyed 10,000 employees. Inadequate recognition is the top obstacle to productivity, according to those studied (49 percent). Reactionary management was seen as the second biggest contributor to the lack of competitiveness (43 percent).[1]

How?

Celebration events, awards, and ideas need to be creative. Having an employee-of-the-month system that becomes routine is not a motivation. Frequently the manager feels compelled to find someone to fill the slot, even if no one stands out.

Individual levels of recognition are well developed in the United States relative to group levels of recognition. Look for ways to reward entire groups.

The most outstanding recognition ceremony I ever attended was spearheaded by Mike Cutchall, the COO of Prism Radio Partners. The ceremony was held in an old, recently restored theater in downtown Jacksonville, Florida. The warm-up was a multimedia bonanza in which music played while smiling employee faces were splashed on a big screen from the year's events. Then, Mike took the stage and very specifically thanked the managers of all 16 stations, listing specific accomplishments from groups and individuals. The speech was peppered with facts and punctuated with applause. At the end of the meeting the group was three feet off the ground. The amount of homework Mike did to be specific and fact based was tremendous. Everybody was a winner, and each mention was a sincere victory. The cost of the celebration was relatively inexpensive ($2000 out-of-pocket expenses). The inspiration generated from the high-quality recognition process was far more powerful than the massive amounts of money sometimes spent on glitz alone.

Who?

The higher the level of the person giving acknowledgment or awards, the more powerful the effect. When I interviewed Marriott reservations people, they talked about Bill Tiefel, the CEO of Marriott Lodging, actually handing them awards. One of the key duties of CEOs and COOs should be recognizing employees' victories.

Tips

1. Look for ways to make everyone winners. In meeting with Toyo Engineering of Japan while I worked at Fluor Daniel, we benchmarked each other. We learned that Toyo frequently had friendly, internal group competitions. Its philosophy was to try to make everyone winners over the long run. Thus, it gave awards for the greatest return on investment, the highest level of creativity, the most effort, the greatest technical innovation, and so on. If one or two groups were winning most of the awards, it would rearrange members in the groups to distribute the

winnings. As Deming said so frequently in his seminars, "You want everyone to feel like winners."[2]

2. Some of the best prizes are those that allow the winners to either showcase their improvement process or learn themselves. Many U.S. and Japanese companies hold quality fairs where contest winners share their successes. Many of the companies with whom I consult offer trips to professional meetings as prizes.

3. Using money as a prize has an inherent drawback. Winners start comparing their prize with others and use the sum to devalue contributions. At Microsoft we had menu-driven prizes where we could choose what we wanted from a catalog.

Motivation Systems: Compensation, Promotions, and Incentives

What Are Motivation Systems?

Motivation systems include performance appraisals, compensation, recognition, and incentive systems for employees. Employees look for tangible ways in which companies communicate priorities. If bonuses and commissions are just based on revenues, that is how employees interpret the relative importance of customer satisfaction and quality.

Why Use Motivation Systems?

Joe Nacchio, CEO of the 1994 Baldrige Award–winning AT&T CCS unit, commented at the 1995 Quest for Excellence Conference that it wasn't until AT&T CCS tied bonuses to customer satisfaction that employees noticed.[3] The high-performing Coca-Cola company ties customer satisfaction results to compensation.[4] A study done at the University of Tennessee by Tom Mentzer queried 185 companies doing customer satisfaction measurement and found that 35 percent had compensation directly tied to the results.[5] More than 24 percent of middle managers had their compensation tied to customer satisfaction. In that same study, Mentzer found even more performance appraisals using customer satisfaction–related goals. Several of the computer, engineering, and insurance companies with which I have worked experienced the same results—it wasn't until motivation systems were tied to customer satisfaction and quality results that the organization started taking the systems seriously.

How?

Compensation can be linked to customer satisfaction and quality on a company, team, or individual level. The company has to determine how critical team involvement is to customer satisfaction. A company like ReMax that is a collection of individual realtors competing with each other does not need team-based compensation plans. A company like Fluor Daniel, Fortune's 1995 Most Admired Engineering Company, for whom I worked for eight years, does. Our sales at Fluor Daniel were always made as a team with engineers, schedulers, a project manager, sales personnel, managers, and others. Team-based rewards are critical in this environment. Fluor Daniel used profit sharing on projects where clients were willing to pay incentive fees for projects well done. Over the life of the project, the incentive fee was distributed throughout the project team based on customer-driven criteria for success. Even part-time secretaries received checks.

Many different types of compensation systems exist in high-performing companies. No one system is the magic bullet. In Japan, compensation tends to be much more homogenous than in the United States. It tends to be structured much more often as a salary plus bonus. Bonuses are based on profits and given yearly. Yearly bonuses are common because Japanese companies don't want employees to raise their standard of living so that the bonus is seen as part of their income. Thus, if the year is not strong financially, the employee will not be dependent upon that income for survival.

In working with several companies on redesigning compensation systems to support customer satisfaction, I have found a couple of things that don't work. Commission-only sales makes it very difficult to service customers. First, commission-only attracts people who may only be solely motivated by money. Salary-plus-bonus pay schemes of many of the Saturn, Lexus, and Infiniti auto dealers support the relationship between compensation systems and service quality.

Transition strategies for changing compensation plans are key. Changing plans frequently and without employee reaction leads to attrition and dissatisfaction. With several of our clients, we found that the commission-only pay system for the sales force was devastating to what the executives were trying to accomplish in customer satisfaction. When the executives first suggested a change to salary plus bonus, the sales force balked. We had to back up and educate the sales force on the relationship between compensation and customer satisfaction. Then we solicited input on how we could change the compensation system to better meet the customer satisfaction goals. The next step involved setting up choices for the salespeople. They were allowed to either keep the status quo or go on to the new structure. Interestingly, the high-producing prima donna salespeople did not choose the new system. The high-producing team players did. We noticed as we looked across the 16 stations owned by the company that revenue increases were directly related to what percentage of the sales force had converted to the new system. Transitions are important to manage.

Performance appraisal at Wainwright is against five key indicators: safety, internal customer satisfaction, external customer satisfaction, six sigma, and business performance. Goals are set individually between the employee and supervisor. Each employee is empowered to make appropriate changes. The quality process is voluntary for all associates but is a major factor in promotions.[6]

Who?

Every employee ultimately has something to do with customer satisfaction. Thus, every employee needs to be part of the motivation efforts. That may mean tying internal customer satisfaction measures to performance appraisals and compensation. That may mean distributing profits among all employees, rather than just the executive level. Wainwright, the previously mentioned Baldrige Award winner, divides the yearly profit *equally* among all employees. Everyone in the company, from the CEO to the janitors, wears the same uniform. The concept is definitely that of a team of equals.

Quality Improvement Teams and Owners

Definition

QITs and improvement process owners are the primary implementers of change. Frequently an owner is given the responsibility and accountability for making the change. A QIT is then chosen to help further define the problem, come up with fixes, and test them. Much has been written about how to use QITs for problem solving. Two reference books are Peter R. Scholtes' *The Team Handbook*[7] and my book *Total Quality Service: A Simplified Approach to Using the Baldrige Award Criteria*.[8]

Benefits

Areas of dissatisfaction for customers will not change by themselves. Having individuals and teams accountable for the fixes is the only way to become a truly customer-focused organization. Customers may be involved in the creative brainstorming of fixes and preventive mechanisms.

How?

Jo Sanders of Wainwright talked about two levels of fixes—the quick fix and preventive action.[9] Within 24 hours of hearing a complaint, an owner is appointed to come up with a quick fix. That containment policy is communicated to the client immediately. An action team then looks at how to prevent the problem from recurring.

Training and Hiring

Definition

Training involves all those activities that develop employees, managers, and executives. It may be an on-the-job mentor program, a classroom experience, or executive development. Training also may be provided for suppliers and customers.

Benefits

Customer-driven training has been highly successful for those who use it. In a needs assessment I did for a radio broadcast company, I interviewed 70 adverisers at five medium-size city locations for their service and advertising needs. The 70 advertisers included retail, beverage, beer, car dealerships, women's apparel, packaged goods, electronics stores, airlines, hotels, insurance, hospitals, banks, mortgage companies, medical products, and others. I interviewed in person and on the phone and found that advertisers wanted help with creative ideas, with putting different advertisers together in catchy campaigns that increased sales. They did not want the "used-car sales" approach that many of the hard-sell salespeople were using. They wanted solutions-oriented salespeople who understood their business. Advertisers had very high standards for what they wanted from the sales force.

That feedback immediately changed training requirements. We had been looking at a Xerox-based program that emphasized closing skills and handling objections. That was just the opposite of what the advertisers were saying was important! We first changed the priority and provided more total quality management training for the general managers and general sales managers of the stations. Advertisers had traced many of their frustrations to policies issued at this level. Secondly, we custom-designed a training program that taught salespeople how to perform needs assessments and analyze business advertising needs. We then taught them how to meet those needs with creative advertising campaigns that worked. We also needed to train customers on how to conduct integrated marketing campaigns. That integration included advertising the customer-perceived strengths of their product, service, or company. It required that customers do their own research and track success better.

Participating advertisers realized a 20 percent to 1200 percent increase in revenue over two years as a result of these programs. Prism, as mentioned earlier, tripled its revenues and market value in that time. These advertisers were true partners. Training was necessary for both employees and advertisers.

How?

Customers can help identify employees' sorely needed training needs. Customer-driven sales and employee training can have a powerful impact on the bottom line. Delta Airlines was faithful about turning service preferences into actual training items for its employees.

Who?

All levels will probably benefit from training after analyzing the customer satisfaction data. The trick is to discern whether an individual, a whole team, or a whole company would benefit from additional training.

Tips

1. Many companies just ask *employees* about their expressed needs for training. Ask customers about what training they would like employees to have.

2. Many strong union environments consider union training as a union problem. Money is allocated for training in specific skills, but sometimes the softer side of success, such as conflict resolution, supervisory training, or communication skills, is missing from the training choices for unions.

3. Performance-based and customer-driven training use real-life situations in the classroom and provide a safe place to practice. Canned programs don't always transfer back to the job. Neither do lecture formats. Thus, training in customer service involves highly interactive role plays, demonstrations and action plans that extend back to employees' real jobs. Training people to fully satisfy customers and yet not give away the store is tricky business. Make sure that training has customer satisfaction accountability.

Likewise, some training ends in the classroom. It needs to thread its way into the daily work of the employee. That can be done by setting goals and monitoring progress over a period of time. Accountability lives at this level.

4. Get customers involved in your employee training. Have customers give kick-off speeches or serve on a panel of judges to evaluate whether the new behaviors are suitable. Most customers are honored and will deepen their partnership with you as a result.

5. Messages about cultural values, quality, and customer satisfaction need to come from the top. The CEO of Ritz Carlton takes two weeks a month to orient new employees to the Ritz Carlton values. Ray Marlow gives the quality orientation for every new employee of the Baldrige Award–winning Marlow Industries. Sales doubled between 1992 and 1995.[10]

6. Pepper your training with customer satisfaction success stories. Those stories carry your message and reward all the hard efforts made by other employees.

7. We see many more customers and suppliers in the training programs we conduct for our regular clients than we used to. The training

needs to be customized to include those partners. I see a high association between gold CSS clients and this increasing tendency.

Visibility Plans

Definition

Visibility plans are plans that determine how you will make the results of your CSS visible. Where will you post results—on bulletin boards, in newsletters, in letters to customers, and so on? Who is responsible for the postings? How often will the results be posted? How will information be reported? How can encouragement be added to motivate employees to higher spirits?

Benefits

One of the profound observations I have had in my six trips to Japan and from observing Baldrige Award–winning companies is how visible the customer satisfaction systems are. Results are everywhere—on bulletin boards, in newspapers, on the lips of supervisors, in meeting rooms, and at individual workstations. The transfer in pride in results comes when results are made visible.

How?

Three levels of data emerge from quality and customer satisfaction measurement systems: individual, team, and company. In Japanese companies, most displays are team or company based. Control charts for individuals were tucked away in drawers for use during performance appraisals. Pitting individuals against each other by posting individual scores leads to peer competition. If teams are important to your success, you may want to move to team-based visibility.

Who?

Visibility plans are best determined by the CSS steering committee. They should be doing the same thing for both quality and customer satisfaction data. See *Total Quality Service: A Simplified Approach to*

Using the Baldrige Award Criteria if you are not familiar with the structural components of a quality effort (like a steering committee).[12]

Tips

1. Get everyone involved in determining what data should be visible.

2. Sort your data to recognize as many people as possible. The same team or set of people should not always be the ones to get recognition. If that is happening, rearrange the teams to spread your winners around. You don't want camps of winners or losers.

3. Set high standards for refreshing data. Old information on bulletin boards and in newsletters makes it look like your process has come to a standstill.

4. Use creativity in presenting data. Marlow has a mural in its cafeteria that depicts the history of the different quality improvement teams. The paths are shown as roads with points at which teams derail (carts are shown tipped over). It helps to make the process fun.

5. Use the visibility to reinforce the use of the system. As was mentioned earlier, Wainwright has a mission control room in which each customer has a chart posted on the wall. Beside that chart is a green flag or red flag. The red flag alerts visitors that the customer satisfaction score has fallen below 95 percent. Jo Sanders, the customer satisfaction manager, said that Wainwright invites customers into the mission control room to see how the data are used. It now has 100 percent cooperation from customers to be interviewed once a month.[11]

Notes

1. "Some U.S. Workers Blame Management for poor productivity," *Quality Progress* 25, no. 5 (March 1992): 14.

3. W. Edwards Deming, speech given at the Optimization of Service Organizations Conference, San Jose, California, 21 July 1992.

3. Joe Nacchio, CEO at AT&T Customer Communication Systems, interview by author, Washington, D.C., 7 February 1995.

4. Tom Fishgrund, group manager of customer satisfaction at Coca-Cola

Company, "Going Global with Customer Satisfaction: It's Not Just a Job, It's an Adventure" (speech given at ASQC's 7th Annual Customer Satisfaction and Quality Measurement Conference, Dallas, Texas, 19–21 February 1995).

5. John T. Mentzer, "Fundamentals of Customer Satisfaction Measurement and Management: What Are Other Companies Doing?" (speech given at ASQC's 7th Annual Customer Satisfaction and Quality Measurement Conference, Dallas, Texas, 20 February 1995).

6. Jo Sanders, customer service manager at Wainwright, interview by author, Washington, D.C., 7 February 1995.

7. Peter R. Scholtes, *The Team Handbook* (Madison, Wis.: Joiner Associates, 1988).

8. Sheila Kessler, *Total Quality Service: A Simplified Approach to Using the Baldrige Award Criteria* (Milwaukee: ASQC Quality Press, 1995).

9. Sanders, interview by author.

10. Ray Marlow, CEO at Marlow Industries, "World Class . . . Wanna Bet?" (speech given at ASQC's 7th Annual Customer Satisfaction and Quality Measurement Conference, Dallas, Texas, 20 February 1995).

11. Sanders, interview by author.

12. Kessler, *Total Quality Service*.

Summary

This book detailed how to design a customer satisfaction system, how to design the tools that support it, and how to use the data. If you are in the middle of this effort, you already know what Tom Fishgrund, the group manager at Coca-Cola expressed so eloquently, "FDR was wrong when he said, 'the only thing you have to fear is fear itself.' Managers also fear customer satisfaction data." The system, the appropriate tools, and a positive system for implementing data take years to develop. You have to take one step at a time. Start with what is cheap and easy—lost customer surveys and doing a better job at complaint resolution. Then move into proactive measures, such as good customer satisfaction measures. Finally, add a creative element and set up tools to really get to know your customers well enough to "invent the future" with them.

The difference to your business customers between the old, traditional way of measuring customer satisfaction (the annual written survey) and a real-time, dynamic, and well-calibrated system is the difference between having a system that is *frightful* and one that is *delightful* to your customers. Competition is too keen to have a CSS that is working against you. When asked whether you can afford to do it right, ask yourself the question, "Can we afford *not* to?" Best practices lead to best-in-class, which leads to best profits—better you than your competition.

Tool Glossary

Advisory board A preselected group of no more than 15 customers that provides in-depth help tailoring your service or product. Usually the board members rotate at least every two years. The group raises issues to research across a broader customer base.

Attrition analysis Calculating the attrition rates and analyzing major events that may have precipitated higher rates of attrition. Typical findings are changes in managers, changes in policies (like return or frequent flyer policies), or changes in internal quality measures of the product/service.

Beta or clinical test or sampling A beta test is used with new service or product launches. For example, software companies ask key customers to use new software for free and report on bugs before the software is released to the general public. A training program may have a pilot for the same purpose. Clinical trials in medicine use the same pilot process to catch problems before a medication is released.

Blind survey *Blind* means that the person surveyed does not know who sponsored the survey. This reduces the temptation for those surveyed to tell you what they think you want to hear. Blind surveys allow you to compare competitors without bias. Good perceptual research usually entails the use of blind surveys.

Cluster analysis Cluster analysis allows the researcher to start with many details and comments in qualitative research and group those details into a few main categories.

Complaint system   A system by which incoming complaints are handled, tracked, and resolved. Results affect the hiring of personnel, training, packaged answers, logging of complaints, and many other features.

Customer event   An event tailored to reach out and touch your customers. The purpose may be to show excitement, showcase new products, promote a customer cause, or just have fun with customers.

Customer information file   A computer-based system of tracking information about customers' preferences and vital statistics.

Customer involvement   Events or ways to get customers involved with co-developing your service or product, such as being an ambassador or providing feedback.

Customer satisfaction survey—telephone   A telephone survey that is usually tailored around how satisfied customers are with different features of the service or product. Questions about expectations as well as perceived performance may be part of the survey. Telephone surveys can also probe areas of satisfaction or dissatisfaction. Telephone surveys allow for greater depth of response than written surveys and create a personal connection with the customer.

Customer satisfaction survey—written   Written customer satisfaction surveys are one of the most expedient ways to have customers quantify their reactions to a limited number of features in your service or product. They are best used when in-depth information is not important or the stakes are low for making errors in your CSS.

Customer training   Training customers in how to install or use your services or products.

Defection measure   A measure of the number of customers who defect. May also provide the percentage of total customers who defect versus those that stay. Same as attrition analysis.

Field study or use study   A field study tracks how customers use your service or product. Field testers may follow the customer for days and watch them use a product. The testers may accompany customers and, for example, watch them drive the truck, use the tool, play with the toy, or work on the software for days at a time. Field studies are becoming increasingly popular. Sometimes usage research is used interchangeably with field studies.

Frequent user program   A program that provides special perks to customers who are frequent customers. The perks may be in the form of discounts, cash awards, extra services, products, or pricing packages.

Intercept study   In an intercept study, people are stopped (usually at the point of purchase) and asked about their buying criteria or satisfaction. Handheld computer intercept devices make it easy to tally the data.

Invent-the-future focus group   An invent-the-future focus group is a specially designed meeting with customers who help you co-invent the next wave of features in your services or products.

Joined-at-the hip programs   Clever companies figure out ways to make their customers depend on them. American Express provides businesses reports on employee spending. FedEx provides shipping software that helps customers track their own packages.

Lost customer survey   Usually a telephone survey of customers who have defected. The format is open ended and usually asks variations of the question, "Why did you leave us?"

Marketing by talking around   This simple yet powerful tool involves training your managers and employees how to ask marketing questions, listen, and record needs in their normal line of duty. The most important point-of-purchase questions are, "How did you hear about us?" "What other companies did you consider?" "What led you to choose us instead of our competitor(s)?"

Moment-of-truth inventory   The inventory is collected in either regular meetings or reports that collect observations from frontline employees on customer needs or complaints. Marriott does this by having each staff group, such as the housekeepers, waiters, and so on, report in monthly meetings about what obstacles are in the way of meeting their mission.

Mystery shopper   A mystery shopper is a researcher disguised as a shopper. These shoppers typically have a checklist of items they look for in the service. Retailers, airlines, and others have used mystery shoppers to check levels of service and how well procedures are followed. Hotels use AAA or Mobil to rate their hotels.

Perceptual survey   A survey that measures customers' perception of your product or service relative to your competition. The pool of sampled customers comes from both your customer and your competitors' customer lists or from potential product or service users. Perceptual surveys are usually blind (see *blind surveys*).

Project review or project audit   A project review or audit is used mainly by project-driven companies, like engineering, telecommunication services, advertising, and so on to assess customer satisfaction during the course of the project. Many times, incentive bonuses are based on these project reviews.

Quality function deployment (QFD)   QFD is an excellent tool to turn customer needs into specifications in the service or product. The tool has been used more in manufacturing than in service, but has made tremendous contributions to both industries. Because several excellent books have been written on this topic, this book will not go into detail on QFD. One excellent book is *QFD in the Service and Administrative Environment* by Kurt Hofmeister, published in 1994. It is available through the American Supplier Institute, 17333 Federal Drive, Allen Park, MI 48101, 313-336-8877.

SERVQUAL   A special type of customer satisfaction survey scale that compares expectations with results. Customers also provide weightings on how important different features are.

Transaction survey   Also known as a *real-time survey*. These brief surveys are done immediately after a transaction (delivery, installation, billing, and so on) and concentrate on the transaction. Usually two questions are central: (1) "What did we do right?" (2) "How could we improve?" Transaction surveys give you a chance to fix the problem on-the-spot—especially if your employees are empowered to make decisions.

Usage research   Investigates what would encourage customers to use more of your product or service. Cellular phone and credit card companies are particularly interested in usage research since the cost of acquiring a customer is high and more frequent use of the cellular phone or credit card considerably increases company profits.

Vital Vision[TM]   Involves training frontline employees to respond to nonverbal clues of satisfaction and dissatisfaction in customers. Employees are trained how to gently encourage customers to verbalize their dissatisfaction so that the employee can fix the problem. This training is important given that only 5 percent of customers actually complain; the rest just walk. Instant problem solving constantly appears as one of the key areas of importance to gold customers in service industries like hotels, airplanes, telecommunications, and distribution companies.

Verbatim analysis   Involves searching for key words or themes within open-ended customer comments. Sometimes verbatim analysis is done through key word searches on computers and sometimes manually with several judges looking for key themes. Verbatim analysis is very important for rolling-up customer-driven compliments or complaints. Cluster analysis is usually performed in conjunction with verbatim analysis.

Warranty card   A card that is returned to the company by a new owner of a product. The card registers the product serial number to the new owner and is a clever way to obtain marketing information. Many companies use these cards to obtain feedback on the buying decision and sales experience of purchase.

Win/loss reports   Typically done after competitive bids with telecommunications, government, engineering, construction, or large competitive manufacturing/supplier contracts awards. Both the winners and losers of the competitive bid interview the decision makers to find out the criteria and rankings.

Bibliography

Armstrong, Larry, and William Symonds. "Beyond May I Help You." *Business Week*, 25 October 1991, 100–102.

"AT&T Ads Cut Confusion." *USA Today*, 15 December 1994, 3B.

Brecka, Jon. "The Gallup 800 Survey Customer Satisfaction Revolution." *Quality Progress* 26, no. 12 (December 1993): 16.

———. "The American Customer Satisfaction Index." *Quality Progress* 27, no. 10 (October 1994): 4.

———. "Good News for Marketers! Survey Says Hire More Marketing Staff." *Quality Progress* 27, no. 12 (December 1994): 16.

———. "The Voice of the Customer Is Loud and Clear." *Quality Progress* 28, no. 5 (May 1995): 4.

Brown, James. "British Airways 'Caress' Passengers with Customer Complaint Program." *Airline Marketing News*, 2 March 1994, 8.

Dutka, Alan. *AMA Handbook for Customer Satisfaction: A Complete Guide to Research Planning and Implementation.* Lincolnwood, Ill.: NTC Business Books, 1994.

Gale, Bradley T. *Managing Customer Value.* New York: Free Press, 1994.

Gordon, Pamela. "Customer Satisfaction Research Reaps Rewards." *Quality* 32 (May 1993): 39–41.

Gross, Neil, and Peter Coy. "The Technology Paradox." *Business Week*, 6 March 1995, 76–84.

Haran, Leah. "Point-of-Purchase: Marketers Getting with the Program." *Advertising Age*, 25 October 1995, 33.

Hayes, Bob E. *Measuring Customer Satisfaction: Development and Use of Questionnaires.* Milwaukee: ASQC Quality Press, 1992.

Hofmeister, Kurt. *QFD in the Service and Administrative Environment.* Allen Park, Mich.: American Supplier Institute, 1994.

"HP's Platt Lauded." *Industry Week,* 19 December 1994, 30.

Jones, E. "Holiday Inns to Spruce Up or Check Out." *USA Today,* 14 September 1994, B1.

Kessler, Sheila. *Total Quality Service: A Simplified Approach to Using the Baldrige Award Criteria.* Milwaukee: ASQC Quality Press, 1995.

Maremount, Mark. "How Converse Got Its Laces All Tangled: It Lost $42.6 Million in 85 Days on Clothing Maker Apex One." *Business Week,* 4 September 1994.

Naumann, Earl, and Kathleen Giel. *Customer Satisfaction Measurement and Management.* Cincinnati, Ohio: International Thomson Publishing, 1995.

Pare, Terence. "How to Find Out What They Want." *FORTUNE,* autumn/winter 1993, 39–41.

"P&G's Aleve Quickly Joins Top Painkillers." *Advertising Age,* 7 December 1994, 3.

Reichheld, Frederick F., and W. Earl Sasser Jr. "Zero Defections: Quality Comes to Service." *Harvard Business Review* (September-October 1990): 106–107.

Ryan, John. "Alternative Routes on the Quality Journey." *Quality Progress* 27, no. 12 (December 1994): 37.

Scholtes, Peter R. *The Team Handbook.* Madison, Wis.: Joiner Associates, 1988.

Sellers, Patricia. "The Best Way to Reach Your Buyers." *FORTUNE,* autumn/winter 1993, 14.

———. "20 Companies on a Roll." *FORTUNE,* autumn/winter 1993, 29.

Stratton, Brad. "Talk to 48,000 Customers Lately?" *Quality Progress* 28, no. 4 (April 1995): 5.

Technical Assistance Research Program. *Customer Complaint Handling in America: An Update Study.* Washington, D.C.: Office of Consumer Affairs, 31 March 1986.

Walther, George R. *Upside Down Marketing.* New York: McGraw-Hill, 1994.

Yovovich, B. G. "High Tech Tools Build New Concept of Market: More Sophisticated Look at Customer Emerges Via Data." *Advertising Age,* 15 October 1995, 25.

Index